NEW DIRECTIONS FOR ADULT AND CONTINUING EDUCATION

Ralph G. Brockett, *University of Tennessee, Knoxville*
Susan Imel, *Ohio State University*
EDITORS-IN-CHIEF

Alan B. Knox, *University of Wisconsin, Madison*
CONSULTING EDITOR

Workplace Learning: Debating Five Critical Questions of Theory and Practice

Robert W. Rowden
Brenau University

EDITOR

Number 72, Winter 1996

JOSSEY-BASS PUBLISHERS
San Francisco

WORKPLACE LEARNING: DEBATING FIVE CRITICAL QUESTIONS OF THEORY
AND PRACTICE
Robert W. Rowden (ed.)
New Directions for Adult and Continuing Education, no. 72
Ralph G. Brockett, Susan Imel, Editors-in-Chief
Alan B. Knox, Consulting Editor

ISSN 1052–2891   ISBN 0-7879-9814-1

NEW DIRECTIONS FOR ADULT AND CONTINUING EDUCATION is part of The
Jossey-Bass Higher and Adult Education Series and is published quarterly
by Jossey-Bass Inc., Publishers, 350 Sansome Street, San Francisco,
California 94104-1342. Periodicals postage paid at San Francisco, California, and at additional mailing offices. POSTMASTER: Send address
changes to New Directions for Adult and Continuing Education, Jossey-
Bass Inc., Publishers, 350 Sansome Street, San Francisco, California
94104-1342.

SUBSCRIPTIONS cost $52.00 for individuals and $79.00 for institutions,
agencies, and libraries.

EDITORIAL CORRESPONDENCE should be sent to the Editor-in-Chief,
Susan Imel, ERIC/ACVE, 1900 Kenny Road, Columbus, Ohio 43210-1090.
E-mail: imel.1@osu.edu.

Cover photograph by Wernher Krutein/PHOTOVAULT © 1990.

♻ Manufactured in the United States of America on Lyons Falls
TCF Pathfinder Tradebook. This paper is acid-free and 100 percent
totally chlorine-free.

CONTENTS

EDITOR'S NOTES   1
Robert W. Rowden

1. Current Realities and Future Challenges   3
Robert W. Rowden
The author introduces the various issues related to educating adults in the
workplace presented in this volume.

PART ONE: WHAT IS THE PURPOSE OF HUMAN RESOURCE DEVELOPMENT?

2. The Purpose of Human Resource Development Is to   13
Improve Organizational Performance
Richard A. Swanson, David E. Arnold
Human resource development should strive to contribute to an organiza-
tion's goals of obtaining effectiveness and efficiency survival minimums by
focusing on employee performance.

3. Development of the Individual Leads to More   21
Productive Workplaces
Laura L. Bierema
A holistic approach to the development of individuals produces well-
informed, knowledgeable, critical-thinking adults who make decisions that
cause an organization to prosper.

PART TWO: IS HUMAN RESOURCE DEVELOPMENT A PART OF
ADULT EDUCATION?

4. Human Resource Development as Evolutionary System: 31
From Pyramid Building to Space Walking and Beyond
Verna J. Willis
The practice of human resource development is neither a new field of study
nor a recent invention, and the field has emerged as an independent entity.

5. Human Resource Development as Adult Education: 41
Fostering the Educative Workplace
John M. Dirkx
The field of adult education is concerned with fostering learning environ-
ments in all situations, including the workplace.

PART THREE: SHOULD THE KNOWLEDGE BASE COME FROM THEORY OR FROM PRACTICE?

6. Professionalization Comes from Theory and Research: 51
The *Why* Instead of the *How To*
Neal E. Chalofsky
Without a reliable theory and research base, a function can never become a
valid field of study with a solid knowledge base.

7. Knowledge Comes from Practice: Reflective Theory   57
Building in Practice
Vivian W. Mott
Knowing comes from doing; a reflective practitioner is a problem solver who
develops theories in use anchored with a practitioner's ways of knowing.

PART FOUR: SHOULD PRACTITIONERS EDUCATING ADULTS IN THE
WORKPLACE BE CREDENTIALED?

8. Human Resource Development Practitioners Should   67
Resist Professional Licensing
Jerry W. Gilley
There are compelling reasons why people who educate adults in the work-
place should resist efforts to become professionally licensed.

9. Human Resource Development Practitioners Should   75
Strive for Certification
Andrea D. Ellinger
Workplace educators should be able to demonstrate certain competencies
and therefore welcome professionalization.

PART FIVE: DO ORGANIZATIONS LEARN?

10. Of Course Organizations Learn!   89
Karen E. Watkins
Human resource development practitioners can nurture and develop the
culture and mechanisms that allow organizations to become hotbeds of
learning.

11. Individuals Who Learn Create Organizations That Learn   97
Victoria J. Marsick, Peter G. Neaman
An organization is made up of individuals, and it is individuals who learn
in the organizational setting.

CONCLUSION   105

INDEX   111

EDITOR'S NOTES

Issues and controversies mark the practice of most professions. This is the case for well-established fields like engineering or medicine, and is especially true for emerging fields such as those concerned with educating adults in the workplace. This volume, *Workplace Learning: Debating Five Critical Questions of Theory and Practice,* presents differing perspectives on some of the most important issues challenging those engaged in educating adults in the workplace so as to inspire improved practice in adult education and human resource development (HRD). An examination of the tensions surrounding adult education and HRD in the workplace can contribute to better understanding and improved practice. The following chapters afford the reader the opportunity to enter the debate and to reflect along with the authors on important questions challenging the field of workplace learning.

In Chapter One, the background and development of workplace learning are presented along with some of the issues that have ensued as the field has emerged from virtual obscurity to its current level of prominence. This chapter provides the context for the issues debated in the chapters that follow.

Part One deals with one of the elementary issues in any field: What is its purpose? In Chapter Two, Dick Swanson and David Arnold argue that a business has a responsibility to maximize stakeholder wealth and that the purpose of HRD is to foster performance improvement. In Chapter Three, Laura Bierema asserts that the development of the individual produces a higher level of employee and leads to more productive workplaces.

Part Two asks a foundational question: Is HRD a part of adult education? In Chapter Four, Verna Willis sees HRD as having emerged from many disciplines and formed its own identity until it now stands apart from its origins. In Chapter Five, John Dirkx holds that although HRD rightly belongs under the larger umbrella of adult education, the goals of HRD must become better aligned with those of adult education.

Part Three looks at an issue that is sure to emerge from any field that is populated by both scholars and practitioners: Should the knowledge base come from theory or from practice? In Chapter Six, Neal Chalofsky argues that ultimately knowledge is formed from research and that quality research must drive the knowledge base of any field. Vivian Mott, in Chapter Seven, supports the view that knowledge comes from practice and discusses the reflective practitioner's ways of knowing.

Part Four examines the need for practitioners to obtain some sort of professional licensing or credential. In Chapter Eight, Jerry Gilley gives compelling reasons why those involved should resist efforts to become professionally licensed, and in Chapter Nine, Andrea Ellinger makes strong arguments for professionalization.

Part Five addresses one of the more recent phenomenons in adult learning, asking the question, Do organizations learn? In Chapter Ten, Karen Watkins discusses many of the group dynamics that support organizational learning. In Chapter Eleven, Victoria Marsick and Peter Neaman argue that an organization is merely a collection of individuals and that it is the individuals in the organization who learn.

Finally, the Conclusion reviews how each of the perspectives illuminates some aspect of the practice of educating adults in the workplace and the ways in which those perspectives intersect and interrelate, revealing a dynamic and diverse arena where both adult educators and human resource developers can engage in reflective practice.

Robert W. Rowden
Editor

ROBERT W. ROWDEN is assistant professor of Human Resource Management and Development and human resources program coordinator at Brenau University, Gainesville and Atlanta, Georgia.

*A number of issues indicative of an emerging field have become evident
as the education of adults in the workplace becomes a major strategic
thrust in many organizations.*

Current Realities and Future Challenges

Robert W. Rowden

Adult learning once was considered a social issue having little to do with business operations (Cook, 1977). However, the influence of overseas competition, new technology, and the changing nature of American employees has made the effective training and retraining of American workers more critical than ever before. The scope of this effort is staggering. Employers spend over $50 billion per year on formal employee training and education. Approximately $180 billion per year is spent on informal, on-the-job training. One in eight workers receives formal employer-sponsored job training each year; this totals an estimated 1.6 billion hours of training for 49 million people (Carnevale and Schultz, 1990; "1995 Industry Report"). In-house human resource development (HRD) departments offer more instruction per employee than such alternative sources as external vendors, educational institutions, labor unions, or trade and professional associations. Without question, the workplace seems to be the catalyst that is changing the nature of adult education ("The Future of Workplace Learning and Performance," 1994).

The importance of all this activity cannot be overestimated. A literate, educated, inquisitive, problem-solving workforce is essential to the survival and competitiveness of business and industry. A labor force that has learned how to learn and continues doing so can give a company a powerful edge.

The last several decades have witnessed tremendous growth in the field or discipline of HRD, but all this attention to workplace learning is not a new phenomenon. Pace, Smith, and Mills (1991) report that as early as about A.D. 1100, crafts training, guilds, and apprentice training were mechanisms for learning in the work environment. With the North American industrial revolution of the

1800s, the emphasis of workplace learning shifted to worker efficiency. The postmodern, or information age has brought about yet another thrust—that of employee enhancement. Today, in most companies, employee enhancement focuses on the worth of the individual employee as a valued human being regardless of the kind of work done or the position held in the organization. With workplace learning evolving as a major strategic thrust in many organizations, the field of adult education and the newer field of HRD both attend to and claim adult learning in the workplace as major areas of study and practice.

Adult Education and Human Resource Development

Watkins (1989) claims that "adult education in business and industry is the fastest growing area of practice in the field of adult education in the United States. Yet as a field of inquiry, adult education in business and industry is relatively young" (p. 422). However, not everyone discusses adult education and human resource development (training and development) in the same breath. Many writers discuss the training and development of workers in the workplace as a field of inquiry separate from adult education.

Attempts are often made to distinguish between training (HRD) and adult education. Some adult educators feel that trainers are not engaged in education. Most trainers believe that they are. Adult educators tend to make this distinction: training is narrow in scope and involves only learning that is directly related to job performance; adult education is concerned with the total human being and his or her insights into, and understanding of, his or her entire world. These attempts to distinguish between HRD and adult education belie the fact that both are concerned with the process of human learning.

Historical context helps explain the divergent development paths of adult education and HRD. Research on adult education can be traced to Dewey's writing and Thorndike's studies of adults in the 1920s. Concurrently, the broad field of practice began professionalizing with the formation of the American Association for Adult Education, publication of seminal materials such as Linderman's *The Meaning of Adult Education* (1926), and establishment of graduate programs to train practitioners in the field. Thus, systematic inquiry dating back to the 1920s helped establish adult education as a bona fide field of study with a solid knowledge base in adult learning. The field of HRD, which also arose out of practice, was not supported by the same type of systematic inquiry until shortly after the Second World War (Wexley and Latham, 1991).

The concept that employers would have to offer some type of workplace learning first emerged in the early 1900s in organizations such as Westinghouse, General Electric, and Goodyear (Swanson and Torraco, 1995), but the idea that workplace learning could help an organization improve effectiveness didn't come to the forefront in North America until around the time of World War II. During that period, the United States had to mobilize all its resources. Vast numbers of men and women entered the Armed Forces, and an even greater number were mobilized into wartime production. However, most of the new workforce had little or no experience in the workplace, especially in manufacturing. It was then that training was seen as a means to easily, efficiently, and effectively give workers the knowledge, skills, and attitudes necessary for production of the vast quantity of wartime materials needed. Many of the methods used to train military personnel were adapted for use in the factories.

The postwar era saw a continuation of the training effort. Although the veterans possessed the knowledge, skills, and attitudes to win a war, they had little knowledge about peacetime employment. It soon became apparent that the same training methods used during the war would be needed a while longer.

Due to the perceived positive effect that training had on the war—and postwar production effort, interest in training was at an all-time high. In 1945, a society for those doing training in organizations was formed. It was called the American Society for Training Directors and later changed its title to the American Society for Training and Development (ASTD). For perhaps the first time since the beginning of the industrial age, systematic research was being conducted on training to determine how to make it more effective and to understand its role in business success. Researchers came from many disciplines, such as psychology, sociology, and business, as well as education and adult education. It is this multidisciplinary approach that has left learning in the workplace wondering where its home really is.

The Purpose of Learning in the Workplace

The job of educating the workforce has come a long way since the 1940s and 1950s. In fact, the focus has shifted from just training to include training and development, career development, organization development, and, to many, organizational learning. The title for the people doing this work has also shifted from simply trainer to the now more encompassing *human resource development specialist* or *manager.*

During the first half of this century, when the workplace was less complex, the mission, or purpose, of the training effort was clear: teach workers how to do their jobs in the most efficient manner possible. The more efficient the worker, the greater the organization's profits. Jobs were broken down to their smallest and simplest components, because workers were thought of as not being very bright. Training was directed primarily toward the cognitive and psychomotor domains (Cranton, 1989). Workers were viewed as easily replaceable cogs in a machine.

Slowly, over the next four decades, things began to change. Signs of the changing times included employers' needs for a more highly educated workforce, even in such traditional companies as steel mills and auto factories. Manufacturing jobs today require that workers have advanced skills in computer technology, robotics, engineering, and communications. The old "tough labor" or hands-on troubleshooting and the need for a strong back are no longer the primary characteristics of American manufacturing jobs. A decade ago, for example, only about 40 percent of production workers held high school diplomas, compared with about 71 percent in 1995. Particularly noteworthy in recent studies by the Bureau of Labor Statistics is the finding that although the size of the workforce doing precision or specialized work has remained nearly constant over the last decade, the percentage of those workers with some college education has increased dramatically (National Coalition for Advanced Manufacturing, 1995).

These changes in the workplace have caused some in the field of workplace learning to examine the goal and purpose of their efforts (Keith and Patton, 1995). Many believe that the purpose of HRD should be performance improvement; others believe that if the focus is on developing the individual, the organization will also benefit.

Those interested in performance improvement usually use the term *human performance technology* and focus on strategies to engineer performance in organizations, including the work processes and organizational systems affecting individual performance. The emphasis is on technical and skills training (Swanson and Torraco, 1995). In this view of workplace learning, management engineering and work processes are stressed.

The other view of workplace learning holds that an individual is the organization. This *individual growth and development* approach holds that workplace learning is a long-term investment in the future of the organization (Cohen, 1994). Any learning opportunities contribute to organizational success by producing a more critical-thinking, problem-solving individual who has the ability to think and act independently in a rapidly changing workplace. Learning-how-to-learn, or lifelong learning, are major themes of this perspective. The concepts of andragogy, first brought to current consciousness by Knowles (1980) in the 1970s, and self-directed learning (SDL) emerge from this principally humanistic perspective, which frames much of adult education. The emphasis is on individual development, independent of work processes.

Development of the Field

It is not easy to define a field of study. It seems that, generally, those in the field of adult education claim HRD as part of adult education, whereas those in HRD attempt to distance themselves from adult education, human resource management (HRM), organizational psychology, and other fields that would lay claim to HRD's purview. Other elements, such as the development of a knowledge base and professionalization, frame the field's boundaries. These elements, in particular, are being examined today for their role in establishing a field devoted to educating adults in the workplace.

With regard to the knowledge base, there seems to be a wide range of opinion as to what type of knowledge should inform the field. Many see HRD as a function populated by practitioners (Rothwell and Sredl, 1992; Goldstein, 1993) and feel that knowing comes from doing. Still others (Campbell, 1989; Latham, 1994) believe that if the profession is ever to be recognized as a legitimate field of inquiry, the knowledge base must be empirically formed.

Those who feel that knowledge comes from practice believe that if one wants to know the best way to do something, one should ask a person who does it. A reflective practitioner is a problem-solver who develops theories in use (Schön, 1983). Those in their ivory towers don't really know what goes on down in the trenches. The only way to ensure a field has a solid foundation is to anchor it with a practitioner's ways of knowing.

The advocates of a more empirically-based field believe that knowledge is formed from research. Without a reliable theory and research base, a function can never become a valid field of study and will forever remain a collection of old wives' tales and speculation. Using all forms of research, both qualitative and quantitative, ensures that a field of study will have a solid foundation. There seems to be little middle ground between the two camps.

There also appears to be little middle ground on another issue related to educating adults in the workplace; namely, licensing or credentialing. There is a contingency that would strongly support requiring that anyone engaged in workplace learning must first be certified by a board empaneled for that purpose or otherwise credentialed (Carlson, 1977; Cervero, 1987; White, 1992). Others contend that because those engaged in educating adults in the workplace are primarily practitioners and the field is still relatively immature, no effort should be made to license or credential those involved (Friedson, 1986; James, 1992).

Those who support the call for certification of HRD practitioners do so out of the belief that it leads to being perceived as professionals, and that society expects professionalism from all practitioners. They contend that in a society where physicians, lawyers, and even plumbers must be certified to practice their trades, educators of adults in the workplace cannot attain the same level of recognition from society until a systematic procedure is in place to ensure a certain level of competence. They also see professional certification as a mechanism for providing standards by which those in HRD can address questions such as who they are, what they are, and what level of proficiency must be attained in order to aid in workplace learning.

On the other hand, the job of educating adults in the workplace is so diverse and changeable, it could be difficult to develop and implement standards of certification. Gilley and Galbraith (1987) have identified three components of professionalization: (1) level of knowledge and competence enhancement, (2) level of importance of occupation to society, and (3) level of control by members of the occupation. Anyone familiar with workplace learning can readily see that the field is nowhere near being a profession based on these criteria. In addition, the issue of accessibility or exclusion must be addressed. If only certified professionals were permitted to engage in educating adults in the workplace, then it is possible, for example, that a supervisor who wanted to conduct a safety training class for a group of coworkers would not be permitted to do so, just as a law clerk is not allowed to represent a client in a court of law. Such a situation would place workplace learning in the hands of professionals—alone. That could mean that nonprofessionals would be barred from sharing their expertise with coworkers, even on an informal or incidental level.

The Learning Organization

These issues are compounded by the recent advent of a phenomenon identified as the *learning organization* (Senge, 1990). A learning organization is generally recognized as one in which learning and work are integrated in an ongoing and systemic fashion to support continuous change and improvement of the organization at the individual, group, and organizational levels. An organization's competitive advantage now appears to evolve around its ability to acquire, use, and generate collective knowledge—in effect, to learn.

The idea of organizational learning has become very attractive to educators of adults in the workplace. The concept of continuous learning in the workplace is seen as a mechanism to finally give credence to the field as the focus shifts from training to learning. It fuels the idea that the whole is greater than the sum of its parts. Educators of adults in the workplace can nurture and develop the culture and mechanisms that allow organizations to become advocates of learning. An organization is like an organism that grows as it learns. Learning comes just as naturally to an organization as it does to an individual.

Yet intuitively it seems that people learn and an organization is nothing without the people. In fact, people are the organization, and learning is an individual thing. The individual learns; the individuals in a group learn; but organizations are not living organisms and cannot learn. Without the people, an organization does not exist. Some view the concept of the learning organization as just another attempt to subvert the individual and make the organization greater than its people.

Regardless of one's position, the idea of the learning organization holds promise not only for organizations but for individuals as well. Such a vision has its basis in both the internal changes that affect the organization and the external changes that affect it as a consequence of an ever-changing environment. That an organization can learn to change is an intriguing idea, with the potential to reform our understanding of competitive advantage and organizational change. If the organization is to survive, it must effect the changes necessary to produce a highly qualified, critical-thinking, and problem-solving workforce that can respond creatively to those changes. At that point, learning becomes the heart of an organization's drive to create and maintain such a workforce. However, it remains to be seen whether the concept of the learning organization is the newest addition in a long succession of management fads.

Summary

The concept of providing learning opportunities for adults in the workplace is not a twentieth century invention. Almost since the idea of work itself, activities of some fashion have occurred to help ensure that workers had the skills they needed. Over the years, a field of study known as adult education began to emerge. Somewhat later, and frantically fueled by the world wars, a specific, multidisciplinary area concerned with workplace learning also began to emerge. This area was identified as training and development, later known as human resource development. The joint, but seemingly separate, development of adult education and HRD has left questions even today as to whether the two fields are in fact the same thing.

Identification and naming are not the only areas of conflict concerned with educating adults in the workplace. Over the years, issues such as what kind of knowledge should inform the field and, in fact, whether or not standards of professionalization or certification should be devised for those involved in educating adults in the workplace have evolved. One recent question facing educators of adults in the workplace is whether an organization can learn, or if an organization is just a collection of individuals and it is the individual who, in fact, learns.

These and other issues may never be settled, for it is this type of scholarly debate that fleshes out a fledgling field and provides it with solid underpinnings. Those on both sides of these debates make very convincing arguments, as can be witnessed in the chapters that follow. As the process of educating adults in the workplace enters the twenty-first century, new issues and challenges will arise. Certainly, the debate will continue.

References

Campbell, J. "The Agenda for Theory and Research." In I. Goldstein (ed.), *Training and Development in Organizations*. San Francisco: Jossey-Bass, 1989.

Carlson, R. "Professionalization of Adult Education: An Historical-Philosophical Analysis." *Adult Education*, 1977, 28 (1), 53–63.

Carnevale, A., and Schultz, E. "Return on Investment: Accounting for Training." *Training and Development*, 1990, 45 (7), S1–S32.

Cervero, R. "Professionalization as an Issue for Continuing Education." In R. Brockett (ed.), *Continuing Education in the Year 2000*. New Directions for Adult and Continuing Education, no. 36. San Francisco: Jossey-Bass, 1987.

Cohen, S. "The Future and HRD." In W. Tracey (ed.), *Human Resources Management and Development Handbook*. (2nd ed.) New York: AMACOM, 1994.

Cook, W. *Adult Literacy Education in the United States*. New York: McGraw-Hill, 1977.

Cranton, P. *Designing Training Programs for Adult Learners*. Toronto, Canada: Emerson and Wall, 1989.

Friedson, E. *Professional Powers*. Chicago: University of Chicago Press, 1986.

"The Future of Workplace Learning and Performance." *Training and Development*, 1994, 48 (5), 529–531.

Gilley, J., and Galbraith, M. "Professionalization and Professional Certification: A Relationship." In *Proceedings of the 28th Annual Adult Education Research Conference*. Laramie: University of Wyoming, 1987.

Goldstein, I. *Training in Organizations: Needs Assessment, Development, and Evaluation.* (3rd ed.) Belmont, Calif.: Brooks/Cole Publishing, 1993.

James, W. "Professional Certification is Not Needed in Adult and Continuing Education." In M. Galbraith, B. Sisco (eds.), *Confronting Controversies in Challenging Times: A Call for Action.* New Directions for Adult and Continuing Education, no. 54. San Francisco: Jossey-Bass, 1992.

Keith, J., and Patton, E. "The New Face of Training." *Training*, 1995, 32 (10), 58–64.

Knowles, M. *The Modern Practice of Adult Education: From Pedagogy to Andragogy.* (2nd ed.) New York: Cambridge Books, 1980. (Originally published in 1970).

Latham, G. "Human Resource Training and Development." *Annual Review of Psychology*, 1994, 45, 545–582.

Linderman, E. *The Meaning of Adult Education.* Montreal: Harvest House, 1961. (Originally published 1926).

National Coalition for Advanced Manufacturing. *What Manufacturing Workers Need to Know and Be Able to Do in Today's Workplace. National Skill Standards for Advance High-Performance Manufacturing.* Washington, D.C.: National Coalition for Advanced Manufacturing (NACFAM), 1995.

"1995 Industry Report." *Training*, 1995, 32 (10), 37–82.

Pace, R. W., Smith, P. C., and Mills, G. E. *Human Resource Development: The Field.* Englewood Cliffs, N.J.: Prentice-Hall, 1991.

Rothwell, W., and Sredl, H. *The ASTD Reference Guide to Professional Human Resource Development Roles and Competencies.* (2nd ed.) Amherst, Mass.: Human Resource Development Press, 1992.

Senge, P. *The Fifth Discipline: The Art and Practice of the Learning Organization.* New York: Doubleday Currency, 1990.

Schön, D. *The Reflective Practitioner.* New York: Basic Books, 1983.

Swanson, R., and Torraco, R. "The History of Technical Training." In L. Kelly (ed.), *The ASTD Technical and Skills Handbook.* New York: McGraw-Hill, 1995.

Watkins, K. "Business and Industry." In S. Merriam and P. Cunningham (eds.), *Handbook of Adult and Continuing Education.* San Francisco: Jossey-Bass, 1989.

Wexley, K., and Latham, G. *Developing and Training Human Resources in Organizations.* (2nd ed.) New York: HarperCollins, 1991.

White, B. "Professional Certification Is a Needed Option for Adult and Continuing Education." In M. Galbraith, B. Sisco (eds.), *Confronting Controversies in Challenging Times: A Call for Action.* New Directions for Adult and Continuing Education, no. 54. San Francisco: Jossey-Bass, 1992.

ROBERT W. ROWDEN *is assistant professor of Human Resource Management and Development and human resources program coordinator at Brenau University, Gainesville and Atlanta, Georgia.*

PART ONE

What Is the Purpose of Human Resource Development?

Human resource development, when practiced in productive organizations, should strive to contribute directly to the organizations' performance goals.

The Purpose of Human Resource Development Is to Improve Organizational Performance

Richard A. Swanson, David E. Arnold

Practitioners and researchers have had a running debate about the appropriate goals of human resource development (HRD). Some argue that HRD should focus on increasing the performance requirements of host organizations and more directly the productivity of the workforce. Others argue that HRD should focus on developing the individual in a broad manner without using bottom line results as the litmus test of an intervention's worth. The question can be rephrased as, What is the dependent variable of HRD? Is it the measurable increase in performance that is the direct result of organizational development and personnel training and development, or is it something else, like individual learning or participant satisfaction with an intervention?

This chapter argues that the purpose of HRD is improved performance. This view is founded on the premise that HRD, when practiced in productive organizations, should strive to contribute directly to the organizations' goals. These goals, based on a purposeful system needing to obtain effectiveness and efficiency survival minimums, are performance-oriented. Consequently, it is the responsibility of HRD to focus on performance. This chapter examines the environment in which organizations operate to gain a better understanding of their goals and responsibilities; discusses the purpose and goals of HRD in that organizational context; and explores the concept of performance to clarify understanding and to demonstrate that the performance versus learning issue may not be a source of conflict.

Organizations in Which HRD Operates

An organization is a productive enterprise having a mission and goals, and it should be thought of as a system, with definable inputs, processes, outputs, parts, and purposes (Katz and Kahn, 1966). With this characterization of an organization in mind, HRD can be thought of as a subsystem that functions within the larger organizational system. To gain an understanding of the purpose of any subsystem, it is instructive to look at the goals of the larger system in which it operates.

One of the first lessons to be learned in any business school is that the purpose of a business organization is to maximize shareholder wealth through the effective and efficient procurement and allocation of scarce resources. This goal of business was not arrived at by chance or by fiat. Instead, it is merely a natural result of the economic and political environment in which businesses function (at least in the United States). In that environment, individuals have the ability to invest money in a variety of vehicles that produce a return. It is natural that investors would want to invest most heavily in organizations that produce the greatest return. The consequence of this is that organizations, in order to attract and retain investors, attempt to provide the greatest returns possible on shareholder investment. Public and nonpublic organizations operate under parallel principles, with their effectiveness and efficiency gains used to reduce costs of services or the expansion of those services. Thus, it is possible to find nonprofits, funded through donations or taxes, outsourcing low-performing subsystems to more competitive, for-profit providers. From these effectiveness and efficiency principles, the goals of profit and nonprofit organizations follow.

Of the scarce resources that organizations must procure and allocate, perhaps none is more important to the success of a firm than human resources. Indeed, one large expenditure for many organizations is tied directly to workers, including wages, benefits, and HRD (Noe, Hollenbeck, Gerhart, and Wright, 1994). Of course, human resources are unique in that people have feelings, make plans, support families, and develop communities. However, human resources are similar to other resources in that firms expect a return on the money invested in them (Cascio, 1987). Unless workers are contributing to the profitability and viability of an organization, then it would make economic sense to invest the money spent supporting those workers elsewhere.

The purpose of reviewing these realities of organizational survival is not to paint an unfeeling picture of the workplace in which people are merely cogs in an industrial machine that operates to line the pockets of greedy investors who do not care about the welfare of workers. There are numerous examples of companies who are meeting their financial goals and are also among the most progressive in terms of employee treatment and relations (Levering and Moskowitz, 1994). Nowhere has it been shown that financial success is in direct conflict with employee happiness and well-being. Instead, these characteristics of organizations were reviewed because they define the organizational system in which HRD operates. By highlighting the purpose and goals of the larger system, insight into the purpose and goals of its subsystems can be gleaned.

The HRD Subsystem

It is difficult to find an article about HRD without at least some reference to linking HRD to the strategic goals of the organization (for example, Gill, 1995). It has become almost axiomatic that if HRD is to develop into a respected and useful player in organizations, then it will need to position itself as a strategically important partner. HRD will need to assume the same level of importance as the traditional core organizational processes: finance, production, and marketing (Torraco and Swanson, 1995).

What are the goals of the organizations with which HRD is to become strategically aligned? As mentioned, ultimately they are survival, return-on-investment, and even growth. More important for HRD, however, are the goals one step removed from these, including producing high-quality goods or services, being the market leader, or having the most highly skilled workforce. Each of these second-order goals serves a singular purpose: to maximize return. The implications of each for the subsystems responsible for carrying them out, however, are more specific and concrete. For example, if it is assumed that the production of high-quality goods is an organizational goal, then production needs to focus on systems and processes that produce quality, marketing needs to focus on systems and processes that communicate quality, and finance needs to focus on systems and processes that ensure quality is supported. And of course, HRD needs to focus on systems and processes that ensure that the individuals in the organization have the knowledge, expertise, and attitudes to produce quality.

Performance is defined as the dependent variable in the form of organizational, work process, or individual contributor outputs of productivity. Using this definition, performance is the means by which organizations achieve their goals. Performance can be measured in many ways. Rate of return, cycle time, and quality of output are three such possibilities. In addition, it is important to make a distinction between levels of performance. Performance takes place and can be measured at the organizational, process, and individual levels.

If HRD should be aligned with the goals and strategies of the organization, and performance is the primary means by which the goals and strategies of organizations are realized, then it follows that HRD should be primarily concerned with improving performance at the organization, process, and individual levels. If HRD is to be a value-added activity of the firm, instead of a line item of cost that is to be controlled and minimized, then HRD practitioners need to be concerned about performance and how it enables organizations to achieve their goals.

HRD and Performance Improvement

How can HRD improve performance? There are many possibilities at the individual, process, and organizational levels. As an example, the mission and goal variables at the organizational level concerns whether the organization's mission and goals fit with various internal and external realities. If they do not, then most likely performance is being impeded. Assume that an organization's mission and goals do not fit the reality of its culture, and that this is resulting in suboptimized performance. HRD could attempt to solve this performance problem through structured intervention in a couple of ways, depending on the outcomes of a detailed analysis. A process could be put in place to formulate a mission and goals that accommodate the organizational culture. On the other hand, a cultural change process could be implemented that seeks to modify the culture so that it is better aligned with the mission and goals of the organization.

Notice that the education of adults plays an important role in this example. If HRD is to change culture, then certainly the principles and practices of adult education will play an important role. It is not difficult to see, however, that there are potential needs for educating and training adults in every cell of the performance diagnosis matrix.

So what is the relationship between HRD and adult education? McLagan (1989) defined HRD as the integrated use of training and development, organization development, and career development to improve individual, group, and organizational effectiveness. Swanson (1994) offered another definition of HRD along similar lines: Human Resource Development is a process of developing or unleashing human expertise through organization development and personnel training and development for the purpose of improving performance. In both definitions, it is apparent that the outcome or dependent variable of HRD is performance.

Another less obvious implication is that HRD is broader than training or adult education. There are HRD interventions that involve much more than training, and some (however rare) that might involve no training at all. For example, HRD might be involved in a business process analysis and improvement that results in a newly engineered process with minor modifications that are transparent to the worker, thus requiring no human resource training for implementation. If training were required, it would be a relatively small part of the entire intervention.

These remarks should not be construed as an argument that adult education is a subset of HRD. It is not. HRD and adult education are discrete entities. Their area of intersection occurs in the host organization. When adult learning decisions about individuals are bounded by the rules and requirements of an organization, adult education becomes HRD. When the rules and requirements are located in the individual, it is adult education. The core test is contained in the idea of locus of control. If the organization retains the authority to approve or disapprove learning interventions, the locus of control is with the organization, and therefore it is HRD. To the point that they are *overtly* shared, they are both.

HRD includes processes and interventions that do not always involve training. By the same token, adult education does not always take place in the context of organizations for the purpose of performance improvement. The outcome or dependent variable of adult education can be personal growth, general knowledge, personal expertise, or even entertainment.

The intersection of HRD and adult education results in performance-focused educational interventions having the following attributes. First, the context is organizations. Second, the dependent variable, or desired outcome, is performance, which will directly affect the goals of the organization. Third, the intersection includes education and training interventions.

Reconciliation of HRD and Adult Education

The tenet that the dependent variable of HRD is or should be performance is by no means universally accepted by practitioners or researchers in the field. Often, concern is expressed that the feelings and worth of human beings are ignored by focusing too much on bottom line results. In addition, some hold that fostering learning or the capacity to learn is a valuable outcome in and of itself and assume that sponsoring organizations will logically benefit. Thus, a line is sometimes drawn between those who view HRD as tied to business goals and focused on the bottom line and those who would like to take a more humanistic stance. This dichotomy is termed the *performance versus learning* debate as a matter of convenience (Swanson, 1995; Watkins and Marsick, 1995).

This debate, like many others, is fueled by an often misconstrued delineation of the opposing sides. On closer examination, it is discovered that perhaps the two sides have more in common than first proposed. On the one hand, those who adhere to the performance orientation of HRD do not do so in an attempt to deny the dignity and worth of employees. Neither do they deny that learning is a necessary component of performance. The goal of performance-focused HRD is simply to ensure that the HRD process in organizations contributes to the goals of the organizational system in which it operates. This does not necessarily imply an authoritarian management style. Some might argue that to ignore performance issues is itself inhumane and inconsiderate of the workforce; good organizational performance does not guarantee job security, but poor organizational performance puts jobs at serious risk. On the other hand, those on the learning side of the debate are not so naive as to think that organizational goals and performance are irrelevant to HRD. On the contrary, they are seen as important, but also important are issues that are difficult to tie to the bottom line of an income statement. Trying to foster a drive to learn in an organization may be a noble goal, but it is one that will be difficult to demonstrate in a cost-benefit analysis. On careful consideration, it appears that HRD and adult education theory and practice may not be in conflict.

Still, it is our contention that HRD should exist for the purpose of improving performance; indeed, it must be performance focused, considering the relationship of HRD to the organizational system it serves. If HRD is to be viewed as a major business process and not just as an optional activity or a waste of resources, then it must be tied to the goals, most of them financial, of the organization. Does this mean that some HRD programs are a priori non-performance-based and thus not worthy of development? No, it does not, and this is an important point that requires further elaboration.

Take developing a learning organization, for example (Senge, 1990). Much has been written lately about the learning organization and the benefits that might come from developing such an entity. To simplify matters, a learning organization is defined here as an organization that fosters long-term learning in the workplace. Using the traditional metrics of performance measurement such as cost-benefit analysis, quality, and cycle time, an increasing number of scholars find it difficult to see how an intervention designed to develop a learning organization could be shown to improve performance (Jacobs, 1995). At least it is not as clear-cut as a program designed to improve the telephone skills of customer service representatives.

Does this mean that there is no place for the development of a learning organization in performance-based HRD? Once again, the answer is no. But the organization must be clear about why it is pursuing such a program and what the expected results are. Sadly, organizations frequently implement ideas and programs without a clear conception of either. This practice is sometimes referred to as *fad-driven HRD. Team building, diversity training,* and *learning organizations* are all concepts many companies develop programs for without a clear idea of why or to what end. If the purpose of HRD is to improve organizational performance, then it is the obligation of HRD to analyze a performance problem in enough detail to determine what the root causes of that problem are and what types of interventions would reasonably be expected to help.

This in no way means that team building, diversity training, and learning organizations do not have a place in performance-focused HRD. If an analysis of an organization's goals shows that such programs would be integral in the process of achieving them, then they should be pursued. By the same token, if a performance diagnosis indicates that the aforementioned programs might be effective solutions, then they should be implemented. What performance-focused HRD does not condone is the blind application of interventions or programs based on whims or poorly conceptualized analyses. Unfortunately, many judge this to be the existing state of the profession. HRD can be irresponsible in its purpose and processes.

Conclusion

What is the dependent variable of HRD? Is it the measurable increase in performance that is the direct result of organizational development and training, or is it something else, like individual learning or participant satisfaction with an intervention?

We have argued that the purpose of HRD is to improve performance. This view is founded on the premise that HRD, when practiced in productive organizations, should strive to contribute directly to the organizations' performance goals.

References

Cascio, W. F. *Costing Human Resources: The Financial Impact of Behavior in Organizations.* (2nd ed.) Boston: Kent, 1987.

Gill, S. J. "Shifting Gears for High Performance." *Training and Development,* 1995, *49* (5), 25–31.

Jacobs, R. L. "Impressions About the Learning Organization: Looking to See What Is Behind the Curtain." *Human Resource Development Quarterly,* 1995, *6* (2), 199–122.

Katz, D., and Kahn, R. L. *The Social Psychology of Organizations.* New York: Wiley, 1966.

Levering, R., and Moskowitz, M. *The 100 Best Companies to Work for in America.* New York: NAL-Dutton, 1994.

McLagan, P. A. "Models for HRD Practice." *Training and Development,* 1989, *43* (9), 49–59.

Noe, R. A., Hollenbeck, J. R., Gerhart, B., and Wright, P. M. *Human Resource Management: Gaining a Competitive Advantage.* Burr Ridge, Ill.: Irwin, 1994.

Senge, P. M. *The Fifth Discipline.* New York: Doubleday, 1990.

Swanson, R. A. *Analysis for Improving Performance: Tools for Diagnosing Organizations and Documenting Workplace Expertise.* San Francisco: Berrett-Koehler, 1994.

Swanson, R. A. "Human Resource Development, Performance is Key." *Human Resource Development Quarterly,* 1995, *6* (2), 207–213.

Torraco, R. J., and Swanson, R. A. (1995). "The Strategic Roles of Human Resource Development." *Human Resource Planning* 1995, *18* (4), 11–21.

Watkins, K., and Marsick, V. "The Case for Learning." In E. F. Holton (ed.), *Academy of Human Resource Development 1995 Conference Proceedings.* Austin, Tex.: Academy of Human Resource Development, 1995.

RICHARD A. SWANSON is professor and director of the Human Resource Development Research Center, University of Minnesota, St. Paul.

DAVID E. ARNOLD is research assistant at the Human Resource Development Research Center, University of Minnesota, St. Paul.

*A holistic approach to the development of individuals in the context of
a learning organization produces well-informed, knowledgeable,
critical-thinking adults who make decisions that cause an organization
to prosper.*

Development of the Individual Leads to More Productive Workplaces

Laura L. Bierema

Workplace learning is in the spotlight as organizations seek leverage in organizational performance. Learning is being heralded as the compass for navi-
gating through an environment constantly pressured by unprecedented
change, competition, technological advancement, globalization, workforce
diversity, reengineering, and downsizing. The recent focus on workplace
learning parallels a shift occurring in the sciences. The scientific community
is in the early stages of a world-view shift, from the machine age to the systems age (Ackoff, 1993). The new sciences have departed from the mechanistic thinking of the old sciences to a more organic understanding of the
world valuing systems, wholes, and relationships. "The essence of the new
science sees the universe as being an undivided whole" (Nordquist, 1995,
p. 2-2). The mechanistic world view has been influenced by discoveries in the
natural sciences dating back to the seventeenth century (Bohm, 1980; Capra,
1993; Wheatley, 1992). The mechanistic perspective, dominant for over three
hundred years, views the world as a predictable, reducible, and controllable
machine. It deeply influenced the industrial revolution, visible in the design
of work from a reductionist perspective where functionalization and simpli-
fication of tasks were primary objectives. Mechanistic thinking can also be
credited with influencing the remarkable success of the industrial revolution,
in the creation of both the assembly line and hierarchical, functional management. Today, there are newer models that are more appropriate for the
challenges of the knowledge and information age. In spite of the availability
of contemporary, more apropos models, organizations continue to apply old
models to new problems.

NEW DIRECTIONS FOR ADULT AND CONTINUING EDUCATION, no. 72, Winter 1996 © Jossey-Bass Publishers

21

Capra calls for a "new vision of reality" (1982, p. 16) because the models we have based social systems on are outdated. The new vision of reality respects the world as an interconnected system of relationships that is interdependent. Senge (1993) echoes this sentiment: "We are in the midst of a worldwide, fundamental shift in management philosophy and practice" (p. 5). The systems perspective recognizes that seeking organizational control is futile. Instead, systems thinkers aim for prediction based on patterns and behaviors over time and recognize that natural systems are self-organizing and that order evolves from disorderly, chaotic processes, such as learning. Harnessing workplace learning has been suggested as a way to shift from the machine age to the systems age mentality. Essentially, making this shift calls for new models of management and workplace development.

A holistic approach to the development of individuals in the context of a learning organization produces well-informed, knowledgeable, critical-thinking adults who have a sense of fulfillment and inherently make decisions that cause an organization to prosper. This, in turn, positively affects society. Of course, organizational environments must also be critiqued for their "conditions of growth" (Dewey, 1916, p. 10). Finally, development must be systemic and holistic if it is to have any lasting effect on either the individual, the organization, or the society.

A new paradigm of individual development is called for in the context of a shifting world view. This chapter presents a case for holistic employee development by reviewing the context of learning and development in the workplace today, exploring the present crisis in individual development in organizational life, and presenting a framework for individual development and organizational development.

Context of Learning and Development in the Workplace

When it comes to workplace management and learning, the machine mentality has been widely applied. Examples include: obsessive growth, rigid management hierarchies, command-and-control management strategies, production-driven decisions, ranking of divisions and employees, rewards for top employees, punishments for low performers, performance heralded as the ultimate goal, internal competition, incentive pay, quotas, short-term focus, reactive management, management by objectives, stifling bureaucracy, and assembly lines. Human resource development (HRD) processes have also embraced the machine mentality exemplified by rigid separation of work and life, quick-fix management gimmicks, reactive behaviors versus creative long-term planning, training unrelated to strategy, training for short-term performance gains, management ownership and control of development, over-reliance on formal training programs, teacher-centered development programs, incremental change, little or no support for personal development or needs assessment, restructuring, and "canned" training. Employee development and work have long been treated as mechanical systems. Yet, the work system is a social system and the mechanical model is beginning to falter.

Capra observes that "the nature of large corporations is profoundly inhuman. Competition, coercion, and exploitation are essential aspects of their activities, all motivated by the desire for indefinite expansion. . . . Corporations work like machines rather than human institutions once they have grown beyond a certain size" (1982, p. 221).

The HRD trend is toward learning organizations, as popularized by Senge (1990). The challenge of becoming a learning organization lies in the ability to truly change the organizational structure of development and management from fragmented, machine-like bureaucracies, to fluid, connected networks. The systems perspective poses yet another challenge for HRD: obsession with the system may distract organizations from focusing on the fundamental aspect of organizational learning and development—the individual. The pivotal task in shifting to a systems model is putting the individual back in development.

Crisis in Individual Development

The machine mentality in the workplace, coupled with obsessive focus on performance, has created a crisis in individual development. Essentially, it has functioned to fragment the person from life. The machine-age organization offers most employees, with the exception of managers and professionals, little control over their workplace activities. Jarvis (1992) emphasizes that "in this organizational and technological world of work individuals learn to become divided selves and to cope with life. . . . Learning how to fit in is a non-reflective learning process" (Jarvis, 1992, p. 180).

There are few rewards in the workplace of today for admitting, "I don't know," or "I need help," or "I might be wrong." Instead, employees are rewarded for competing against each other, having the right answers, and moving quickly in moments of crisis. This reward system leaves employees with little or no time to reflect on the consequences of their decisions or actions. Work is less than fulfilling and employees are meeting personal development needs outside the workplace. One need look no further than the newspaper comic strip *Dilbert*—a comic strip created by Scott Adams that bemoans the dehumanizing, unmotivating, controlling workplace of modern life—to sense that something is amiss in organizational life.

Organizations, in their infatuation with the quick fix, pour money into development when it affects the bottom line and when times are good. Yet development that is solely productivity-based misses what it means to be human. There is such an epidemic lack of systems thinking in organizations today that the suggestion of whole-person development will be received by many mechanistic managers as absurd. However, "earning and living are not two separate departments or operations in life. They are two names for a continuous process looked at from opposite ends. . . . A type of education based on this vision of *continuity* is, obviously, the outstanding need of our times" (Lawrence P. Jacks excerpt from *Journal of Adult Education,* 1929, pp. 7–10 in Knowles, 1990, p. 32; emphasis in original).

A shift from economic growth to inner growth is desperately needed. Korten, author of *When Corporations Rule the World,* in a keynote address at the 1996 Academy of Human Resource Development, observed that "the evidence is accumulating that we face a problem that can be resolved only by changing the structures, the rules of the game, of the larger economic and political system within which business operates" (p. 2). People work to serve higher purposes, both tangible and intangible. Thus, systemic workplace development offers a unique opportunity for learning and education that affects lives, work, and communities. In the words of Dewey, "an occupation is a continuous activity having a purpose. Education *through* occupations consequently combines within itself more of the factors conducive to learning than any other method" (1916, p. 308; emphasis added).

Valuing development only if it contributes to productivity is a viewpoint that has perpetuated the mechanistic model of the past three hundred years. In the systems perspective, this viewpoint is counterintuitive. New models of individual development, which link the whole individual to the organization and society, are in order. Although not without risk, the new model holds great promise for individuals and organizations alike.

Framework for Individual Development

Although mechanistic workplaces and development processes are insensitive to adult development across the life span, the theory and practice underlying adult learning and systems thinking offer alternatives. Holistic individual development for the future is grounded in humanism, systems thinking, and adult learning theory. Merriam and Caffarella observe that "learning in adulthood is an intensely personal activity" (1991, p. xi). Yet, organizations function to depersonalize, organize, control, and often constrain workplace development.

Merriam and Caffarella also estimate that 90 percent of the population is involved with at least one self-directed learning activity a year (1991, p. 54), and Marsick and Watkins (1990) observe that much of the learning in the workplace is either incidental or unintended. What is known about adults as self-directed learners is that they need personal autonomy, they have the willingness and ability to manage their own learning, they need a context that gives them control over their learning, and they meet learning goals without the use of formal institutions or methods (Candy, 1991). In spite of this, much of the development that occurs in the workplace is formal, productivity-based, and fragmented.

Managers who believe that employees are motivated only to serve the corporate interest or who are willing to invest only in development that clearly affects the bottom line are missing the opportunity to capture the natural energy and enthusiasm that adults bring to their personal learning. They are also likely to be entirely ignoring the reality that their employees are engaged in learning that is meaningful to the organization with or without management support. What organizations must recognize is the cost of not investing in individual development. Unfulfilled employees are less productive and often leave the organization. The long-term cost of replacement is prohibitive to any employer.

What is the bridge that links individual and organizational development? Systemic thinking offers tools and models to build this bridge. Capra believes that "what we need therefore, is to revise the concept and practice of work in such a way that it becomes meaningful and fulfilling for the individual worker, useful for society, and part of the harmonious order of the ecosystem. To reorganize and practice our work in this way will allow us to recapture its spiritual essence" (Capra, 1982, p. 233).

Employees deserve the space and support to create and articulate a personal vision and understand how it connects to the organizational purpose and goals. This demands that the organization create an infrastructure promoting holistic individual development and then connect it on a collective level. This infrastructure supports giving employees the space to reflect and plan safely, and share discourse with other people in the organization about plans and goals.

To suggest that individual development in and of itself is the total answer would violate the very principles of systems thinking. It is the place to start, but once it has been cultivated, it must be integrated into the organization if it is to benefit the learning of other employees and the productivity of the organization. Mumford (1996) suggests a pyramid of learning that begins with individual learning at its base followed by one-on-one learning, progressing to group or team learning, and culminating in organizational learning. The hierarchy suggests that organizational learning cannot happen without the preceding levels of learning. The critical understanding lies in the linkage between individual and organizational learning and ways of synthesizing the two. The systems model of development demands an infrastructure that promotes individual growth, commits to cultural change, and strategically links individual and organizational growth.

Promoting Individual Growth. Organizations are made up of people. Holistic development integrates personal and professional life in career planning, development, and assessment. Holistic development is not necessarily linked to the present or future job tasks, but the overall growth of the individual with the recognition that this growth will have an effect on the organizational system. Dewey asks, "How can there be a society really worth serving unless it is constituted of individuals of significant personal qualities?" (1916, p.121).

Merriam and Caffarella (1991) conclude that adults engage in learning for the sake of learning, and holistic development essentially involves giving adults the space and support to learn. The ultimate challenge in organizations is to harness adult learners' propensity to be self-directed learners and not create barriers that prevent or discourage it. Senge (1990) refers to the process of individual development as "personal mastery" or "the discipline of personal growth and learning" (p. 141). Personal mastery is the art of defining current reality accurately while concurrently holding an image of a vision that is desired. Senge suggests that the higher the level of personal mastery, the higher the level of commitment, responsibility, and motivation in the organization. Customized, personalized employee development is a dramatic shift from the bottom-line production based focus of the mechanistic age. Making the shift not only requires an ardent commitment to individual development, but also a shift in the culture of the organization.

Culture. An organization is made up of people who have relationships and share values. The culture of an organization deeply affects the day-to-day functioning of the organization. To shift into the systems perspective, the traditional culture must be challenged, a shared vision for systemic development must be cultivated, and a commitment to long-term change must be made.

Workplace development has followed the machine age mentality. Yet, change is in the air. Block reflects, "I think the field of workplace learning and performance is going to return to the person and the individual and to building community and participation. . . . Learning and performing will become one and the same thing" (1993, p. 38). Dodgson (1993) argues that "individuals are the primary learning entity in firms, and it is individuals which create organizational forms that enables learning in ways which facilitate organizational transformation" (pp. 377–378). Senge argues that taking a stand for full employee development is a radical departure from the traditional contract between employee and institution; in fact, it might be the most radical departure in a learning organization.

Individual development and performance are not either-or options in organizations today. Performance will improve with individual development actions, but the culture must also support it. Senge notes that "ironically, by focusing on performing for someone else's approval, corporations create the very conditions that predestine them to mediocre performance. Over the long run, superior performance depends on superior learning" (1990, p. 7). To achieve renewed focus on individual development and foster a culture change, organizations must design infrastructure to support the learning, or systems, world view.

Infrastructure. An organization is made up of people who are bound by a shared structure and context. Fritz (1989) argues that structure determines behavior and that true change evolves only from creating new structures that are more supportive of the desired outcome. Learning occurs all the time. The task is to ensure that effective learning is happening. Watkins and Marsick (1993) observe that "transformation will not come if learning functions as a parallel system, as the training system function does now" (p. 20). Because structure determines behavior (Fritz, 1989) the present mechanistic structures have not supported whole individual development. Osterberg notes that "in the old way of thinking, companies exist primarily to make profit. In the new way of thinking, companies exist primarily as structures within which people come together to create cooperatively" (1993, p. 69). Osterberg also notes that the hierarchical structure is a serious obstacle to personal development because it is built on fear and mistrust. The current process of goal setting is debilitating as well, because it prevents personal development by removing the chance to take divergent routes on the way to achieving organization vision.

Organizations should also develop models of learning that allow them to practice and document their learning processes. A systems perspective, to recognize how jobs relate to each other and to the overall performance of the firm, is also a necessary ideology. Firms must recognize that only through relationships does anything get done and to cultivate strong relationships throughout the organization is a key performance strategy. A company is not a machine but a living organism. Thus, living policies will be much more effective in cultivating an environment that encourages holistic development. The task for human resource developers is to help organizations understand the systemic long-term benefit of creating structures to support that kind of development.

Conclusions

The process of linking learning to performance needs extensive inquiry. Assessing the link between learning and performance is difficult. Nadler and Nadler (1992) note that "learning brings about the *possibility* of a change in performance" (p. 84), and Crossan, Lane, White, and Djurfeldt (1995) conclude that "there is no evidence to suggest that learning is synonymous with improved performance. . . . Conversely, good performance is not necessarily a sign that learning has occurred" (p. 353). Almost every adult works, and understanding the learning in this context is of fundamental importance to adult educators. Convincing organizations to support a systemwide strategy is difficult.

Adult educators and human resource development professionals are uniquely equipped to research, design, and implement new models of workplace development with the individual and learning as top priorities. Clearly, the challenge for adult development in the workplace calls for new models. Bergevin (1967) captures the spirit of whole-person learning:

> Adult education must, then, have a purpose greater than that of learning the skills of the craftsman and the physician and the entrepreneur, important as those are. If we are truly engaged in the maturity process, we do not live to work and make money, or have a physician keep us alive merely to be alive. We learn what to do with our lives, how to use our money and our good health to enrich our lives. We use these resources, money and education and health, to help us live. A significant task of adult education is to teach us how to live a full, productive life in which the ability to make a living and stay well is important, but equally important is the knowledge of what to do culturally and spiritually with our lives and talents. [p. 41]

The systems age demands that organizations foster and support individual development in the workplace for the long term. Such development will have a lasting positive effect on individuals, organizations, and the society as a whole.

References

Ackoff, R. "From Mechanistic to Social Systemic Thinking." Paper presented at the Systems Thinking in Action Conference, Boston, September 1993.

Bergevin, P. "The Adult, His Society, and Adult Education: An Overview." In S. B. Merriam (ed.), *Selected Writings on Philosophy and Adult Education*. (2nd ed.) Malabar, Fla.: Krieger, 1995.

Block, P. *Stewardship*. San Francisco: Berrett-Koehler, 1993.

Bohm, D. *Wholeness and the Implicate Order*. London: Ark Paperbacks, 1980.

Candy, P. C. *Self-direction for Lifelong Learning*. San Francisco: Jossey-Bass, 1991.

Capra, F. "A Systems Approach to the Emerging Paradigm." In M. Ray and A. Rinzler (eds.), *The New Paradigm in Business: Emerging Strategies for Leadership and Organizational Change*. New York: Putnam, 1993.

Capra, F. *The Turning Point: Science, Society and the Rising Culture*. New York: Bantam, 1982.

Crossan, M. M., Lane, H. W., White, R. E., and Djurfeldt, L. (1995). "Organizational Learning: Dimensions for a Theory." *The International Journal of Organizational Analysis*, 1995, 3 (4), 337–360.

Dewey, J. *Democracy and Education: An Introduction to the Philosophy of Education*. New York: Free Press, 1916.

Dodgson, M. "Organizational Learning: A Review of Some Literatures." *Organization Studies*, 1993, *14* (3), 375–394.

Fritz, R. *The Path of Least Resistance*. New York: Fawcett Columbine, 1989.

Jarvis, P. *Paradoxes of Learning: On Becoming an Individual in Society*. San Francisco: Jossey-Bass, 1992.

Knowles, M. *The Adult Learner: A Neglected Species*. Houston: Gulf, 1990.

Korten, D. "When Corporations Rule the World." Paper presented at the Academy of Human Resource Development Conference, Minneapolis, Minn., March 1996.

Marsick, V., and Watkins, K. *Informal and Incidental Learning in the Workplace*. London: Routlege, 1990.

Merriam, S. B., and Caffarella, R. *Learning in Adulthood*. San Francisco: Jossey-Bass, 1991.

Mumford, A. "Building a Learning Pyramid." In K. Watkins and V. Marsick (eds.), *In Action: Creating the Learning Organization*. Alexandria, Va.: American Society for Training and Development, 1996.

Nadler, L., and Nadler, Z. *Every Manager's Guide to Human Resource Management*. San Francisco: Jossey-Bass, 1992.

Nordquist, H. E. "The New Paradigm of Human Resource Development: A Holistic Model." In E. Holton (ed.), *Proceedings of the Academy of Human Resource Development*, 1995.

Osterberg, R. V. "A New Kind of Company with a New Kind of Thinking." In M. Ray and A. Rinzler (eds.), *The New Paradigm in Business: Emerging Strategies for Leadership and Organizational Change*. New York: Putnam, 1993.

Senge, P. "The Art and Practice of the Learning Organization." In M. Ray and A. Rinzler (eds.), *The New Paradigm in Business: Emerging Strategies for Leadership and Organizational Change*. New York: Putnam, 1993.

Senge, P. "The Leader's New Work: Building Learning Organizations." *Sloan Management Review*, 1990, *32* (1), 7–23.

Watkins, K. E., and Marsick, V. J. *Sculpting the Learning Organization: Lessons in the Art and Science of Systematic Change*. San Francisco: Jossey-Bass, 1993.

Wheatley, M. *Leadership and the New Science*. San Francisco: Berrett-Koehler, 1992.

LAURA L. BIEREMA is residency network director in the College of Human Medicine at Michigan State University and adjunct faculty in the Office of Medical Education, Research, and Development.

PART TWO

Is Human Resource
Development a Part of
Adult Education?

Human resource development is modeled as an evolutionary system
with an incumbent professional identity. Accepting this model changes
the rules for professional practice, field description, and field theory
development.

Human Resource Development as Evolutionary System: From Pyramid Building to Space Walking and Beyond

Verna J. Willis

A wide, sweeping search for new and enhancing ways to think about human resource development (HRD) is likely to be a hallmark of HRD practice and professional preparation in the twenty-first century. It is not that HRD is frail or depends on this kind of professional soul-searching for its life support, but rather that HRD is growing so fast and in such interesting variety that it draws attention. There are volumes still to be learned about the HRD person (the HRD self), about HRD work and its effects, and about HRD as a field. Perhaps this quest for deeper understanding signifies a coming of age.

Almost certainly, HRD will not revert to its earlier powerlessness and will not be treated as an organization stepchild, as it has been in the past (Baird, Schneier, and Laird, 1983). The HRD search for its place is now being internalized as reflection on personal experience and hope for the future. Externalized, the search gradually crystallizes in the form of a detailed intellectual and performance history of HRD. In retrospect, the contributions of many perspectives from multiple root disciplines are instructive, spelling out the life work of valued theory-builders and practitioners (Underwood, 1991). But now there is an urgent need to acknowledge HRD as a confluence, an intermingling of disciplines that produces something new.

HRD as Confluence

The confluence of disciplines in HRD appears to have reached flood stage, spreading over the globe and into space as astronauts from worlds apart fly off to learn from each other. What the future of HRD becomes may have every-thing to do with what practitioners and academics currently think it is, and further, whether they will acknowledge a sense of belonging to it. Collective action on behalf of HRD as a field, and HRD status as a discipline, depend on such perceptions and commitments.

The HRD milieu is richer now than ever. This may be an effect of a pri-mary though often misunderstood principle of general systems theory: that the whole is greater than the sum of its parts. Most people relate this princi-ple to the idea of synergy, and that is where it stops. What may be a more important aspect of the principle is that a confluence of systems produces something other than the sum of its parts. Another point often missed is that *greater* means added elements plus changed configurations. It does not imply *better* unless new elements are systemically integrated, contributing to effi-cacy of the whole. A confluence analogy is useful for showing the *other than* nature of whole systems. Even though the Missouri River, the Ohio River, and other tributaries are watershed systems in their own right, downstream they are part of a mighty confluence. The larger whole, the Mississippi River system, began in many places including its own river source, and it is more than the sum of its tributaries. It is also distinctly different from any of them, and different from what it once was. Metaphorically, HRD is like the Missis-sippi, downstream from its origins and its contributing disciplines. It is a whole new river.

To attempt even a simple listing of root disciplines is hazardous, for HRD theorists and practitioners will take from whatever disciplinary sources they need at any given time. Nevertheless, there is considerable agreement that adult education; instructional design and performance technology; psychol-ogy; business and economics; sociology; cultural anthropology; organization theory and communication; philosophy; axiology (study of values); and human relations theories, principles, and practices have all become a visible part of the HRD milieu.

Pulling HRD apart and trying to restore elements of it to various disci-plines—for example, by implying that it can be factored into organization development, career development, training and development, or other elements—is like saying that the waters of the Missouri, the Ohio, and other tributaries can be separated and made distinguishable after they enter the Mis-sissippi. Historical reviews of the root disciplines and of HRD system growth are finally beginning to show how much exchange there has been and how lit-tle any one discipline can claim to have originated or to hold the high ground of HRD.

The difficulty for those in HRD who maintain strong identifications with their root disciplines is that, although they can travel overland or chug upstream to their roots, they are forever changed by their trip downstream. The HRD river experience does not wash off. Fortunately a systems thinker can acknowledge belonging to the HRD profession without chopping off sus-taining roots. Every HRD practitioner or professor has honorable lineage from somewhere else. Clinging excessively to lineages, however, may do violence to what HRD has become: a new system of thought and practice that has its own identity and professional incumbency.

Take the case of performance technology. From its inception as an instructional development strategy to deliver better training, it has grown to encompass organizational analysis and consulting dimensions. It may not even lead to training, but to something else that helps individuals and technical systems work better. Enlarging also, career development has become the task of every employee and every manager-coach. Organization development has become deeply embedded in productivity issues without losing its interest in the learning power of group experiences. Adult education has both feet in HRD practice, although reflexively it seeks knowledge about how people learn. Vocational education still leans to the technical training side, but has recently begun to correct toward more comprehensive prework education.

A thorough analysis of the root disciplines just mentioned—and many others that have made HRD so richly multidisciplinary—might show marked differences in underlying assumptions about people and how they work. Different paradigms (world views) are certainly present in these fields. The point is, however, that not only practice but also theory making about practice seem to be flowing together at a faster rate than ever before.

So it seems that HRD as a coming together of disciplines has already happened. What remains is not only for practitioners and academics to acknowledge this but also to recognize HRD as a powerful, boundary-flexing, evolutionary system. It will change in the future, as it has in the past, but quite likely at an even faster rate. What it must respond to is a startling deficit: a learning rate in organizations running far below the rate of need for learning (Revans, 1982).

As it evolves, HRD may need a new name to represent itself more accurately and to escape from limiting images. Names are powerful, and one denoting systemic organizational learning (SOL) might do more to acknowledge the widening band of constituencies and also emphasize the quantum leaps required to accomplish learning at the rate of change (LRC). But name-change is speculative. Less controversial is the need for widening the HRD angle of vision to acquire a more panoramic view of what people in twenty-first century organizations will need. The learning required for pyramid building has never been fully explained and still elicits awe. How much more mysterious, and how daunting, are the learning tasks of the future!

Systematic Plus Systemic Thinking and HRD

Because this chapter encourages study of HRD as an evolutionary system with built-in professional identity, a thumbnail sketch of systems thinking may help. Terms from general systems theory have crept into every kind of science and social science literature over the past three decades. Some of the original meanings seem to have been lost along the way, leaving misconceptions.

Banathy's systems education classification (1972) specifies four levels of systems analysis and language. Most "systems talk" in HRD appears to be at technician or technologist levels, not at levels of field theory or theory about general systems. Often when a so-called systems approach is applied, it turns out to be largely systematic, as in instructional systems design (ISD) or much of performance technology. These are tool-using, tool-making activities that proceed in relatively linear though often highly creative fashion. The branching sophistication of contemporary multimedia and the Internet tells the power of technician-technologist levels of systems thinking. Even so, this sophistication appears to be more systematic than systemic. A definition of systematic is "methodical in procedure or plan, marked by thoroughness and regularity, [and] of, relating to, or concerned with classification, specifically taxonomic" (*Webster's Collegiate Dictionary,* ninth edition).

Systemic thinking, used to develop field theories and explain systems of relations in HRD, is much rarer. Again by Webster's definition, systemic means "of, relating to, or common to a system; specifically, affecting the body generally." This comes much closer to what von Bertalanffy had in mind when he first described the common properties of systems in organic terms (1968).

Recognizing that field theory in HRD is itself undernourished as the twentieth century draws to a close, there is already the challenge of addressing the general system level of theory development previously bypassed. Literature relevant to this effort could include such matters as explaining and changing organizational thinking and action in terms of systems complexity, chaos, or creativity. Climbing up Banathy's ladder of systems thinking from immediate actions to systemic knowledge about HRD takes its advocates steps beyond *how to* and toward questioning *what* and *why.* As the field of HRD matures, this would seem to be where it ought to head to help people in organizations learn at the rate of change.

Evolutionary Systems Thinking and HRD

Seven years ago, Peter Senge thoughtfully reminded everyone that systems thinking is a core discipline (1990). But systems thinking is anything but new; it is evolutionary and at least as old as tool making. It draws heavily on intuitive, personally constituted modes of knowing and deliberately merges science and art. Somehow, people learned together how to build all kinds of impressive systems, from pyramids to astronomical calendars. In the Middle Ages, scholars conceived and modeled systems elements and the workings of the entire universe. Such complexes of meaning, part fact and part belief, infuse all knowledge.

Scientific respectability for systems thinking arrived with the formation of the Society for General Systems Research in 1954. Von Bertalanffy's general theory about systems and his subsequent elaborations were inspired efforts, for out of them grew unprecedented cross-fertilization of ideas and the beginning of a knowledge revolution that is still in progress. General systems theory provides researchers and practitioners with a metalanguage and metaconceptual framework for studying whole systems, irreducible to component parts.

Flood (1990) has argued that systems science engenders three complementary methodological positions: positivistic, interpretivistic, and critical or ideologically based inquiry. All three points of view are visible in journals like *Systems Practice, Systems Research,* and *Complexity.* Philosophically, these are all subsumed by evolutionary systems theory, which examines systems like ecology, growth limits, and bifurcations that represent choices between the kind of world systems humans can consciously create and the kind of world that will arrive by default if nothing is done (Laszlo, 1991). At its best, HRD may bridge the gulf between what is (roads now taken) and what might be: the world acting as a system evolving simultaneously toward progressive integration and differentiation, with *working together* becoming the norm. At the same time, each person is accorded individuality and there is considered to be value in diversity. Variety is required for healthy systems.

Systems either evolve and become something wholly new, or they disappear, and in so doing release energy and resources for other, more viable systems. This is not only the essence of evolutionary systems thinking but also of paradigm changing, for old paradigms tend to hide new ways of seeing and creating (Kuhn, 1967; Wheatley, 1992).

Pyramid-Building: HRD Beyond Disciplines, Roles, and Outputs

Reframing ideas about HRD has often taken the form of modeling. Despite the trend toward more complex and systemic definitions of the field, a mind-set remains that HRD is part of, though peripheral to, human resource management (HRM). A model slightly removed from this is McLagan's human resource wheel (1989a) showing HRD outside human resource management, divided into three parts, and doing collaborative work with HRM. Although the wraparound idea of HRD is preferable to versions that show HRD as marginalized by organization maintenance tasks of HRM, the wheel is still bound up in issues of the status quo (Watkins and Willis, 1991). With slight variations, other authors have followed McLagan's lead. For example, Pace, Smith, and Mills (1991) have suggested analytical, developmental, instrumental, and mediational roles for HRD, but also kept eleven subroles from the McLagan model. McLagan herself suggested that there is a need for matching systems theory to future HRD issues (1989b).

Some recent HRD books (for example, Swanson, 1994; Brinkerhoff and Gill, 1994) are thoughtfully framed in systems language. Still, because they are technician-technology oriented, they are more systematic and taxonomic than systemic, as previously defined. They do not lead directly to construction of field theory in HRD or general theories about HRD as an open system. Chalofsky and Lincoln earlier found five major perspectives on HRD: conceptual/philosophical, operational, functional, field of study, and field of practice (1983). The conceptual or philosophical view seems least represented in current writing, and yet it is the "growth stock" of the future.

Several practitioner-theorists do make this kind of investment. Watkins, for example, has modeled HRD as a collection of metaphors, rather than a collection of disciplines, and has asked for the hearing of "many voices" in the debates over what HRD is or may yet be (1989, 1991). Watkins and Marsick (1993) offer an extended model for action in the learning organization. It is worth watching for other articles and books that make heavy use of conceptual modeling; they bode well for the ongoing development of field theory. If the motif of learning is at the heart of HRD and of organizational change, then it needs to be displayed as such in newer models and the contributions of adult education theory need to be made more explicit.

Spacewalking: HRD as a System for the Future

An attempt to conceptualize HRD as a system began during the design of a university core curriculum in human resource development (Willis, 1989). Avoiding the existing systematic, taxonomic patterns in that turning-point year meant that, while wading in a sea of competencies produced by eleven different studies in the United States and Canada, a gestalt switch and paradigm shift was necessary. To describe HRD as an integrated system with interacting elements and a whole new life of its own seemed a good way to move beyond technician-technology levels of system thinking.

The first requirement for redefining a system is to rethink system boundaries. In this case, a circle of HRD is scribed wholly apart from HRM. Such a step is supported by historical precedents, systems science itself, and practitioner experience confirming that HRD and HRM belong to different "paradigmatic continents," Flood's (1990) term for widely differing points of view. Willis and May (1996) contend that HRD is spinning off from HRM just as management information systems (MIS) were earlier spun off from finance departments. In each case, the subsidiary has become too important to be left for last.

Adult education also forms a spin-off that is too important to be left for last. Once it was thought to be a slight and even capricious variation on mainstream teaching and learning theory and practice. Adult learners themselves—in great numbers—have decided otherwise. In a world where the rate of learning falls far behind the rate of change, adult education theory and practice have emerged as necessities that offer a rich vein of ore for understanding and practicing HRD. Research that reveals adult learners as meaning-seekers and self-transformers also shows that learning in organizations goes far beyond task behavior change.

When professionals move from adult education academic programs into practice in organizations, they join the "Mississippi" of HRD, even though they do so in a way that fits their own world view most closely. This is not different from what happens to HRD practitioners who draw strength from other root disciplines. Each stream makes its own contribution and forms its own relations in the HRD system. The fact that those who have experienced HRD have an urgent and practical interest in action learning and creating learning organizations seems a case in point.

The second requirement for understanding HRD as a system is to see that it looks and operates like a system. An initial model was presented to HRD professors nationally in 1990, proposing that if HRD is conceived as a whole system (symbolized by a three-dimensional sphere) and if it is cut in cross-section across any diameter, five things (elements of action) are occurring at any given time. These are instructing, advising-coaching, designing, managing, and consulting. Each is distinguished operationally. This overrides the troublesome problems of role and discipline differentiation, for everyone in HRD is always doing all of these things, whatever specific form each action takes.

What this model enables is the description of what actually happens in HRD, no matter what the academic lineage, position title, or level of expertise of the practitioner. It is in and around this general system of responsibilities that HRD curriculum emerges without violating any of the prior taxonomies. This picture has been helpful to those entering the field from other disciplines, acting as proof that they can transfer root concepts, skills, and values to the HRD profession.

Figure 4.1 is not what it seems; it only masquerades as a matrix. It is actually an open file cabinet that may be missing any number of fat, relevant files. For example, the whole category called Action Learning has sprung up since last filing. Another set of files is piling up in international HRD. The aim of this symbolic cabinet is not to be encyclopedic but to illustrate how an HRD practitioner works with information when engaged in any of the five system action sets or when researching foundation literatures. Crossovers happen routinely, for any action may involve some or all other actions.

HRD, like Figure 4.1, is not a finished, closed system; it is evolving and open to further description. It needs to become much more self-aware if it is to have a greater effect. HRD needs to have its feet planted firmly on the ground in order to break out in space and cyberspace. It is an incredible achievement to have come so far and done so much for people in organizations, even after discounting for failures. It is launched toward a future for people who work, learn, and care for each other in a seamless way. Chances are that it persists and has shown itself as such a complex system simply because it accredits the unslakable human thirst for lifelong learning.

Figure 4.1. File Cabinet for Human Resource Development

Foundations	Instructing: delivery	Advising and coaching	Designing	Managing or leading	Consulting (peer)
Systems and structures	Lesson planning; organizing	Employee development	Performance technology	General models and philosophies	Organization development; change orientations and philosophies
–General systems	Stand-up strategies	–Career access and development	–ISD; other models	Management career paths	–IT and ID
–Psychosocial systems	–Teaching and learning styles and modes	–Mentoring	–Front-end analysis	HRD careers	–OD
–Management systems	–Methods, techniques, and settings	–Mobility	–Template-making for analysis, design, implementation, evaluation of all varieties of training and development	HRD management	–Training and development
–HRD systems	–Learner involvement and internalization	–Asset-based manpower planning and use		–Reporting relations	–CD
–Systems, allied fields	Brain/mind strategies	–Outplacement		–Central or decentralized	–MBO
Models and paradigms	–Accelerated Learning	Workplace issues	Mediated teaching and learning strategies, tools	–Administration systems	–Corporate culture
HRD general and field	–Imaging, metaphor	–Political, social, economic climate	–Hypermedia	–Training and development systems	–Ergonomics
–Assumptions	–Cognitive process	–Interpersonal effectiveness	–Hypertext	–Strategic vision	Empowerment strategies and structures
–Theories	Computer deliveries	–Ethnic, gender diversity	–AI	–Planning; proposals	–Participative management
–Definitions	–CBT, CAI	–Equity	–Other computer media	–Executive presentation; other communication	–Reticular work groups
–Ideologies	–Videodisc, video	–Autonomy; power	–Other media	–Marketing	–Flat and hierarchical
HRD traits, skills, and certification	–Learning systems	–Literacy	Sociotechnical systems	–Staffing, supervision	–Sociotechnical strategies and accommodations
HRM and HRD distinctions	–Tutorials	–Parental leave	–Productivity and quality systems	–Performance monitoring	–Other power shifts
New technology	–Automated processes	–Child care	–Communication and reporting systems	–Contracting, brokering services	Transfer of change agentry skills to organization
–Automation	Evaluation strategies	–Health care and fitness	–Accountability systems	HRD finance	Research and writing
–Software	Applications, follow-up	–Access to training and development	–Employee involvement and participation	–Budget	Professional associations
Globalization	Varieties of training	–Access to employee assistance programs		–Cost/benefit analysis	
Productivity; quality	–Sales	–Layoff, termination		–Profitability	
Work and society	–Customer service	–Violence		–Corporate accounting	
	–Technical	–Work rules		–Financial reports	
	–Supervisory			–Forecasting	
	–Management			HRD image	
				–Internal	
				–External	

References

Baird, L. S., Schneier, C. E., and Laird, D. *The Training and Development Sourcebook.* Amherst, Mass.: Human Resource Development Press, 1983.

Banathy, B. "A Systems Analysis of Systems Education." *Educational Technology,* 1984, *12* (2), 421–439.

Bertalanffy, L. von. *General Systems Theory.* New York: Braziller, 1968, 1972.

Brinkerhoff, R. O., and Gill, S. J. *The Learning Alliance.* San Francisco: Jossey-Bass, 1994.

Chalofsky, N., and Lincoln, C. I. *Up the HRD Ladder.* Reading, Mass.: Addison-Wesley, 1983.

Flood, R. L. *Liberating Systems Theory.* New York: Plenum, 1990.

Kuhn, T. S. *The Structure of Scientific Revolutions.* Chicago: University of Chicago Press, 1967.

Laszlo, E. *The Age of Bifurcation: Understanding the Changing World.* Philadelphia: Gordon and Breach, 1991.

McLagan, P. A. *Models for Excellence: The Models.* Alexandria, Va.: American Society for Training and Development, 1989a.

McLagan, P. A. "Systems Model 2000: Matching Systems Theory to Future HRD Issues." In D. B. Gradous (ed.), *Systems Theory Applied to Human Resource Development.* Alexandria, Va.: American Society for Training and Development, 1989b.

Pace, R. W., Smith, P. C., and Mills, G. E. *Human Resource Development: The Field.* Englewood Cliffs, N.J.: Prentice-Hall, 1991.

Revans, R. *The Origins and Growth of Action Learning.* Bickley, Kent, UK: Chartwell-Bratt, 1982.

Senge, P. *The Fifth Discipline.* New York: Doubleday, 1990.

Swanson, R. A. *Analysis for Improving Performance: Tools for Diagnosing and Documenting Workplace Expertise.* San Francisco: Berrett-Koehler, 1994.

Underwood, L. P. "On the Shoulders of Giants: The Evolution of Management Training and Development." *Dissertation Abstracts International,* AAC 8919876, 1991.

Watkins, K. E. "Five Metaphors: Alternative Theories for Human Resource Development." In D. B. Gradous (ed.), *Systems Theory Applied to Human Resource Development.* Alexandria, Va.: American Society for Training and Development, 1989.

Watkins, K. E. "Many Voices: Defining Human Resource Development from Different Disciplines." *Adult Education Quarterly,* 1991, *41* (4), (Summer), 241–255.

Watkins, K. E., and Marsick, V. J. *Sculpting the Learning Organization.* San Francisco: Jossey-Bass, 1993.

Watkins, K. E., and Willis, V. J. "Theoretical Foundations of Models for Practice—A Critique." In N. M. Dixon and J. Henkelman (eds.), *Models for HRD Practice: The Academic Guide.* Alexandria, Va.: American Society for Training and Development, 1991.

Wheatley, M. *Leadership and the New Science.* San Francisco: Berrett-Koehler, 1992.

Willis, V. J. "A Function-Based HRD Curriculum." Monograph. Atlanta: Georgia State University, 1989.

Willis, V. J., and May, G. L. "The Chief Learning Officer: A Case Study at Millbrook Distribution Services." *Proceedings of the Academy of Human Resource Development,* Minneapolis, 1996.

VERNA J. WILLIS is associate professor of human resource development at Georgia State University.

Human resource development needs to move away from its reliance on the market model as a way of framing its practice and embrace the democratic ideal represented in the tradition of adult education.

Human Resource Development as Adult Education: Fostering the Educative Workplace

John M. Dirkx

Many years ago, as a health care worker, I found myself in an in-service workshop on operating fire extinguishers, an educational event required for all hospital employees in order for the hospital to maintain its national accreditation. As I entered the large auditorium, my name was checked off on a list. For the first half hour, we listened to firefighters talk about fire safety. Then, in small groups, we went outside, where controlled fires were purposefully set in wastebaskets. After the experts demonstrated how to use the different extinguishers, we practiced on the wastebasket fires. We were then certified on the use of fire extinguishers. Several days later, few of us remembered what extinguishers to use on which fires or how to use them.

Work-related education and training occupies a curious intellectual space in the broader landscape of adult learning. According to a recent report, 33 percent of employed adults in the United States receive some form of job-related training (U.S. Department of Education, 1994), and work-related goals are the most common reason given for adults participating in some form of education (Courtney, 1992; Merriam and Caffarella, 1991). Yet, as educators of adults, we don't know quite what to make of this form of learning. The practice of human resource development (HRD) is a case in point. Adult educators themselves disagree as to whether HRD should be considered a part of their field. Seeing themselves as upholding the vision of the field of adult education articulated many years ago by Lindeman (1926, 1961), some decry the encroachment of vocationalism on a field traditionally committed to social justice and the empowerment of people (Hart, 1992; Collins, 1991; Cunningham, 1993). Others tend to view HRD as a legitimate area of practice within the broader field of adult education (Brookfield, 1986; Watkins, 1989). Although HRD specialists generally regard their field as ultimately committed to the corporate bottom line, they, too, disagree as to whether their practice is best understood as a form of adult education. Some see it as virtually interchangeable with adult education (Nadler, 1984); others argue that it represents a field of practice distinct in many ways from adult education (Gilley and Eggland, 1989; Willis, this volume).

The economic aims and purposes of HRD have been used by HRD specialists as well as critical adult educators to distinguish the field from the practice of adult education. HRD continues to be influenced by an ideology of scientific management and reflects a view of education where the power and control over what is learned, how, and why is located in the organizational leadership, corporate structure, and HRD staff, a view of education clearly illustrated in the opening vignette. In many respects, this in-service program is typical of many kinds of workplace education and training programs. Humanistically-minded reform efforts have done little to fundamentally alter the ways work and the workplace are conceptualized. Recent writings, however, in work and organizational life emphasize the developmental function of work and the participatory and democratizing trends in the workplace, both of which are challenging the fundamentally economy- and job-centered framework in which much of the practice of HRD is cast. The democratic and social justice traditions of adult education provide HRD with a conceptual framework for guiding its practice in these new workplaces.

"It's the Economy, Stupid": Market Economy and HRD

The traditional hallmark of an HRD program is its relationship to the sponsoring organization, a relationship usually defined in economic terms. This orientation is not surprising, given the pervasiveness of the market model in the way we think about society and our lives. In a jacket-cover endorsement of a popular book on supply-side economics (Wanniski, 1989), former President Ronald Reagan wrote, "Economic truth is a lever that can move governments, move history . . . the economic model that we've created truly has become . . . the way the world works." When responding to a question about his salary, former Chrysler executive Lee Iacocca remarked, "That's the American way. If little kids don't aspire to make money like I did, what the hell good is this country?" (DeYoung, 1989, quoted in Kincheloe, 1995, p. 121). Workers in the 1992 Democratic presidential race were reminded of the key issue in the campaign with the centrally located motto "It's the economy, stupid."

Although one goal of adult education is to strengthen the forces of democracy in society, HRD is often conceptualized and justified within a market economy model, reflected in the various assumptions embedded in its practice. The market model is grounded in a view of humans as *homo economicus*, "a human who is primarily an instrument for economic aims" (Kincheloe, 1995, p. 5). Individuals work to live—to consume—and the meaning of work rests with its capacity to provide workers with this consumptive power. The job is viewed as being composed of distinct, specifiable skills and competencies that are empirically demonstrable and separate from the individual who performs them. Effective performance is determined by measuring the value added to the corporate bottom line. The conditions of the workplace and the kind of work individuals are asked to do are considered only if they influence the efficiency with which an individual worker acquires the knowledge and skills necessary to perform the job.

Evolving from the scientific management movement (Taylor, 1911), practitioners of workplace learning programs have adopted a language of technical rationality for framing their work and "scientific" strategies for planning learning experiences and assessing their effectiveness. Learning in this context is intended to contribute, through improved performance, to the bottom line and, ultimately, to our society's global competitiveness. In the traditional view of HRD, practitioners focus on designing and implementing programs that transmit to passive workers the knowledge and skills needed to improve the company's overall performance and, ultimately, society's economic competitiveness. In this market-driven view of education, learning itself is defined in particular ways, largely by the perceived needs of the sponsoring corporation and the work individuals are required to perform.

As a result of this job-centered, bottom-line orientation, value is placed on some forms of learning, and other forms are marginalized. For example, a welder participating in a twenty-hour workplace literacy program targeted to improve his job-related reading skills remarked, during a break in instruction, that he really wasn't learning anything from the program and that "if they taught me how to read, now that would be something." He wanted to be able to read stories to his grandchildren and this program was not helping him accomplish that goal. With such an emphasis on predefined, formal learning, nonformal and incidental learning goes largely unnoticed. When asked what they have learned from their work, workers often refer to such lessons as the power structures in the workplace; what a person *really* needs to do to get ahead—whom to please and whom to ignore; and the minimum amount of work they need to do to avoid being fired. HRD practitioners work hard to effectively package knowledge in predefined behaviors and skills, whereas workers are busy constructing their own meaning of work. They learn to see their workplaces as authoritarian, mind-numbing, fragmented, repetitious, monotonous, dreary, and often unsafe (Kincheloe, 1995; Terkel, 1974).

HRD specialists and critical adult educators point to the market-based approach as a major reason why HRD should be considered apart from adult education. This position, however, is untenable, not only for the ethical issues involved but because it does not adequately conceptualize the emerging view of work described in the literature and increasingly acted on by companies. This perspective is consistent with the individual and social justice traditions of adult education, traditions based on the idea that economic well-being *follows from* rather than *produces* a strong and vibrant democracy (Kincheloe, 1995).

Framing HRD Within the Tradition of Adult Education

The emerging paradigm reveals a view of work that is developmental, participatory, and self-authorizing, if not democratic. Considerable emphasis is placed on contextual or situational learning, in which worker-learners are collaboratively engaged in both problem-posing and problem-solving. As Welton (1991), points out, these qualities are educative and contribute to a sense of the workplace as a primary site for adult learning and the practice of adult education.

Although new to the workplace, these characteristics reflect a long-standing moral and political tradition in adult education. In the first part of this century, Lindeman (1926, 1961) argued that an individual's life is largely shaped by the institutions, politics, and economics of the times. For Lindeman, the meaning of adult education rested with its capacity to work for and help fully realize a democratic vision in society. Such a form of education was characterized by four assumptions that have come to be well known among adult educators today: (1) education is life, rather than a preparation for it; (2) the purpose of education is to add meaning to life and provide opportunities for individuals to express themselves rather than merely train individuals to perform specific functions; (3) the emphasis in adult education needs to be on the specific contexts in which adults find themselves, focusing on learners' needs and interests rather than subject matter; and (4) the most important resource in the learning setting is the individual's experience, which is, as Lindeman stated, "the adult learner's living textbook" (p. 7).

Lindeman's ideas formed a core set of assumptions about how adults learn, which many educators of adults today know as *andragogy*. Popularized by Knowles (1980), andragogy also became part of the lexicon of workplace learning. This reinterpretation of Lindeman's ideas, however, cast adult learning in an individualistic framework. Many workplace educators adapted these principles to social and political contexts structured largely to honor the corporate bottom line rather than fostering the broader, democratic vision inherent in Lindeman's ideas. As a result, much of HRD and workplace education assumes a traditional schooling quality, with emphasis being placed on what is to be learned. Process issues are considered as technical strategies to achieve predefined goals and objectives, in which workers have relatively little voice. Although the so-called quality improvement effort was hailed as a new approach to involving workers in more democratic decision-making processes, many workers perceived interventions such as quality circles as little more than impotent structures designed to garner worker support and rubber stamp decisions already made by organizational executives. Self-managed teams are a recent reincarnation of this approach to "democratizing" the workplace, and they are floundering in many organizations for similar reasons. Reducing process issues to a kind of technical intervention ignores the profoundly different view of social and political relations that is inherent in more worker-centered ideas. Rather than being viewed as ends in themselves, they become means to ends that are largely economic and have little to do with fostering individual development or strengthening democracy. In other words, HRD has been implicitly conceptualized by many practitioners as contributing to the smooth functioning of the corporate machine, a kind of educational lubricant to increase the efficiency and effectiveness of existing goals and structures. Andragogy has simply become pedagogy with an adult twist.

But the vision that Lindeman and others held for the field of adult education has not been abandoned in the workplace. Many researchers and practitioners recognize the andragogical qualities inherent in good work and continue to work for full implementation of these principles. In various ways, adult educators such as Brookfield (1986), Marsick (1987), Watkins (1991), and Mezirow (1991) redefined the meaning of andragogy by emphasizing the importance of fostering critical thinking, critical reflection, and other learning-to-learn strategies. The work of Watkins and Marsick, both of whom see themselves as adult educators, has had an especially profound influence on revitalizing these ideas of adult learning in the workplace. Critical educators, however, argue that even these attempts to reform the concept of andragogy fail to take workplace education and training beyond their individual-centered approaches (Collins, 1991; Cunningham, 1993; Hart, 1992; Welton, 1991, 1995). But even critical educators do not devalue the importance of the individual's experience of work. For example, Kincheloe (1995) argues that a critical postmodern pedagogy of work involves "an image of a just future grounded on a description of good work" (p. 66). Good work, according to Kincheloe, involves a sense of completion and fulfillment, an engagement with the individual's meanings and purposes. Welton (1991) argues, "The empirical evidence from work and personality studies certainly suggests that good work is a normative need for human beings" (p. 41). By good work Welton suggests a content of work that provides "opportunities for development of worker wellbeing" (p. 32). In exploring subsistence work, Hart argues for a view of work that "acknowledges rather than denies the natural foundation of human existence," an understanding of work as oriented "towards use and life" (1992, p. 177).

The process issues so prominent in the emerging views of work are also prominent facets of adult education practice. Rather than predefining the goals of workplace learning through some kind of scientific or technical strategy, an HRD practice guided by the vision of adult education for democracy would emphasize what Welton (1991) refers to as the "educative workplace," in which worker-learners together define what it is that is meaningful and significant to learn.

HRD practitioners, as well as managers and supervisors, assume more of an "enabling" role (Welton, 1991) in this environment and become resources for the worker-learners. In this model, more attention is given to the kinds of work individuals are asked to perform and the ways in which that work is structured and organized. These issues provide opportunities for workers to engage in thoughtful, meaningful, and critical ways of learning and influencing their work environments. When HRD is framed within the context of the emerging paradigm of work and as a form of adult education, it will then see itself as being about the business of fostering learning environments in the workplace.

When conceptualized as a form of adult education, the practice of HRD can make significant contributions to transforming workplaces into truly educative environments. I agree with Brookfield (1986) that adult educators should become more aware of HRD as a form of educational practice; however, the future of HRD needs to be informed by the tradition of adult education committed to furthering a just and democratic society. In such a model, the HRD manager's motto might be, "It's the democracy, stupid."

References

Brookfield, S. D. *Understanding and Facilitating Adult Learning.* San Francisco: Jossey-Bass, 1986.

Collins, M. *Adult Education as Vocation: A Critical Role for the Adult Educator.* London: Routledge, 1991.

Courtney, S. *Why Adults Learn: Towards a Theory of Participation in Adult Education.* London: Routledge, 1992.

Cunningham, P. M. "The Politics of Worker's Education." *Adult Learning,* 1993, 5, 13–14.

Gilley, J. W., and Eggland, S. A. *Principles of Human Resource Development.* Reading, Mass.: Addison-Wesley, 1989.

Hart, M. U. *Working and Educating for Life: Feminist and International Perspectives on Adult Education.* London: Routledge, 1992.

Kincheloe, J. L. *Toil and Trouble: Good Work, Smart Workers, and the Integration of Academic and Vocational Education.* New York: Peter Lang, 1995.

Knowles, M. *The Modern Practice of Adult Education: From Pedagogy to Andragogy.* Chicago: Association Press, 1980.

Lindeman, E. C. *The Meaning of Adult Education.* Norman: University of Oklahoma, 1926, 1961.

Marsick, V. (ed.). *Learning in the Workplace.* Croom Helm: London, 1987.

Merriam, S., and Caffarella, R. *Learning in Adulthood.* San Francisco: Jossey-Bass, 1991.

Mezirow, J. *Transformative Dimensions of Adult Learning.* San Francisco: Jossey-Bass, 1991.

Nadler, L., (ed.). *The Handbook of Human Resource Development.* New York: Wiley, 1984.

Taylor, E. *The Principles of Scientific Management.* New York: Harper & Row, 1911.

Terkel, S. *Working.* New York: Ballantine, 1974.

United States Department of Education. *Adult Education: Employment-Related Training.* Washington, D.C.: Office of Educational Research and Improvement, 1994. NCES 94–471.

Wanniski, J. *The Way the World Works.* (3rd ed.) Morristown, N.J.: Silver, Burdett & Ginn, 1989.

Watkins, K. E. "Business and Industry." In S. B. Merriam and P. M. Cunningham (eds.), *Handbook of Adult and Continuing Education.* San Francisco: Jossey-Bass, 1989.

Watkins, K. E. *Facilitating Learning in the Workplace.* Geelong, Australia: Deakin University Press, 1991.

Welton, M. R. *Toward Development Work: The Workplace as a Learning Environment.* Geelong, Australia: Deakin University Press, 1991.

Welton, M. R. (ed.). *In Defense of the Lifeworld: Critical Perspectives on Adult Learning.* Albany, N.Y.: SUNY Press, 1995.

Willis, V. "Human Resource Development as Evolutionary System: From Pyramid Building to Space Walking and Beyond." In R. W. Rowden (ed.), *Workplace Learning: Debating Five Critical Questions of Theory and Practice.* New Directions for Adult and Continuing Education, no. 72. San Francisco: Jossey-Bass, 1996.

JOHN M. DIRKX is associate professor of higher, adult, and lifelong education and associate director of the Michigan Center for Career and Technical Education, Department of Educational Administration, Michigan State University.

PART THREE

Should the Knowledge Base Come from Theory or from Practice?

Without a solid theory and research base the discipline will never become a valid field of study but will forever remain a collection of anecdotes and speculation.

Professionalization Comes from Theory and Research: The *Why* Instead of the *How To*

Neal E. Chalofsky

The first trainers did not see themselves as pioneers in a new field, but as professionals in other fields who had a job to help adults learn a specific skill (Nadler, 1990). Human Resource Development (HRD)was not even seen as a significant activity until World War II. (Although the oldest training association, the Training Officers' Conference, was started by federal government training officers in 1938.) During this time, the armed forces and the industrial establishment were desperate for competent personnel. It was discovered that vast numbers of the adult population were capable of being trained and made productive in relatively short periods of time. Since that time, the overwhelmingly major focus of the field has been to provide services through the development and delivery of training programs.

The basis for developing these programs has been a mixture of guesswork, trial and error, and the borrowing of theory and research results from other disciplines. The trial-and-error approach seems to have usually been chosen over a study of theory and research. The only theory adhered to was Knowles' adult learning theory. Examining what is considered best practice in the field is a relatively recent phenomenon, and this approach still begs the question of whether what works in one context will work equally well in another. This is not to say that there are no practitioners who have tried to develop programs and interventions based on theoretical constructs or solid research findings. But, as a percentage of the total practitioner pool, they would be an infinitesimal number.

NEW DIRECTIONS FOR ADULT AND CONTINUING EDUCATION, no. 72, Winter 1996   © Jossey-Bass Publishers

There is no question that up until recently, HRD, like adult education, has been a practical and applied discipline. According to Jensen, "Its [adult education's] primary objective is coping effectively with some unsatisfactory state of affairs or problem of everyday life" (1964, p.106). Jacobs (1990) echoed this theme when he stated that "HRD is both an area of professional practice and an emerging interdisciplinary body of academic knowledge. The interrelatedness of these two aspects makes HRD similar to most other applied professions, most of which have emerged to meet some important social or organizational need. After the practice is established, the need arises to formalize the knowledge gained in practice into some logical structure. Such activity helps legitimize the profession and increases the reliability of practice" (p.66).

This structuring began in 1967 with the publication of an article by Lippitt and Nadler and continued in 1976 (Bureau of Training) with the first national research study devoted to identifying the roles and competencies of HRD specialists (from one sector; the federal government). The structuring ended with the most recent role and competency study conducted by the American Society for Training and Development (ASTD) (McLagan, 1989).

HRD's Current Body of Knowledge

Every new occupation seeking professional status has sought to delineate its foundation in terms of its unique body of knowledge (Jarvis, 1987). HRD, again like adult education, has developed a unique body of knowledge suited to its purposes through two methods: experiences gained from coping with problems of practice lead to the formulation of principles or generalizations that provide guidance for future practice; and knowledge that has been developed by other disciplines is borrowed and reformulated for use in the field (Jensen, 1964). The current body of knowledge is still represented by the ASTD study mentioned earlier. The results of this study represent both practice and borrowed theory and knowledge, which is sometimes hard to distinguish because of the mingling of the two over the years. The data collection technique used to arrive at the results was to poll approximately three hundred "experts" (as identified by a committee of practitioners and academics) as to what they perceived to be the critical roles and competencies for the HRD field in five years (from the time of the study). This may be a legitimate form of inquiry for a field in its infancy, but it does not translate into a full-fledged body of knowledge for a professional discipline. There has been little, if any, research to test the experts' perceptions; few attempts to develop theoretical constructs from the data; and almost no scholarly critique and debate of the value of the study beyond its immediate applications (except Dixon and Henkelman's *Academic Guide to the Models for HRD Practice*, 1991.)

Is this role and competency model really enough to provide a foundation, or core, for the discipline to build from as it matures as a profession? If the core is the area where the discipline's own theory and practice will emerge, it should contain the following:

Philosophy and mission. The essence of why this field exists as a profession; its purpose, values, and the ethics that provide the foundation for the professional practice of the field. The notions of helping adults learn in work settings and optimizing human and organizational growth are philosophically-laden terms that represent a value toward the development of human potential.

Theory and concepts. The intellectual underpinnings of the profession. If the philosophy represents the heart of the field, the theory represents the brain. This is the basic knowledge needed to function as professionals. Jacobs (1990) cites education, systems theory, economics, psychology, and organizational behavior as the five major disciplines that have most influenced the field, although he admits his list is by no means exhaustive. Other disciplines such as sociology, anthropology, and management science have been mentioned as contributing to the theory base (Chalofsky and Lincoln, 1983). Although there seems to be general agreement that the field works from an interdisciplinary body of theory, there is no agreement as to what part should be considered essential for HRD professionals. Whether the theory is generated from within the field or borrowed from other disciplines, the field needs to continue to build a theoretical foundation.

Roles and competencies. The heart and brain need the body in order to implement the ideas they generate. The profession needs a core set of skills and abilities in order to put the theories and concepts into practice. Dixon and Henkelman's recent (1991) study actually identified fewer roles than McLagan's (1983) study, even though the scope of the study was broadened. The eleven roles identified by McLagan were further organized into the four roles (learning specialist, manager, consultant, and career development specialist) that have been in the literature since 1975 (Chalofsky, 1989). Those in the field are also aware of the competencies that could be considered core to the discipline; the ones that are most often required for performance of the roles only need to be identified. Enough research data has been compiled to provide for day-to-day practice at present.

But abstract sets of competencies are not enough to guide professional practice. Consider Lewin's well-known formula: behavior is a function of the interaction between performance and the environment (Watkins and Willis, 1991). Professionals may know what needs to be performed, but they know little of the social context (the organizational environment) where the performance will operate or the psychological context (the individual inner environment) of the learner. Those in the field need to develop the theory and conduct the research that will translate the results of this study into truly professional practice.

Failure to Professionalize the Field

Professionals know what roles should be performed and are continually scanning the field for best practice, but the field has yet to reach the level of a mature profession for the following reasons.

What we practice is based on guesswork, not on theories tested by research. Most of what is practiced in the field is still, at best, educated trial and error and is often the fad of the month. Few organizations or HRD consulting firms conduct research to test new approaches. And the academic research being conducted is still too new to stand the test of being translated into practice.

What we practice is at least ten years behind the state of the art, in terms of both research and thinking. Emerging research and theory building is approximately five years ahead of the state of the profession; (what is considered best practice in the field). The state of the profession is approximately five years ahead of the state of practice (what usually goes on in organizations on a day-to-day basis). This is true of most professions; physicians prescribe treatments they are familiar with until a new one is brought to their attention by various professional sources. And they read their journals and go to conferences to keep up with the latest research. They are aware that each level pushes the one below it and it is their responsibility to be aware of what is going on at each level to give their patients the best service possible.

In HRD, the state of research and theory building did not have outlets for dissemination until several years ago, with the establishment of the *Human Resource Development Quarterly* and the *Performance Improvement Quarterly*. In addition, an association for HRD academics (the HRD Professors' Network of ASTD) was established in 1981 but did not seriously begin to promote scholarly work until the Academy for Human Resource Development was formed in 1993. Thus, research and theory building has not been guiding or informing day-to-day practice. Instead, we have had people's opinions and ideas cloaked as new theories driving practice.

What we practice is based on what the client wants, rather than on what works. As a helping profession, HRD is unique. The field is not guided by a professional set of standards, expected to adhere to an enforceable code of conduct, or committed to a philosophically based professional mission or set of professional values. The field is context- and situation-based. Some would say this is beneficial, because it allows us to be flexible enough to deliver the services needed by our clients. But it also means that we deliver the services and interventions our clients want but do not necessarily need. Professionals may know what the client needs and what interventions will work, but what ultimately gets delivered is what sells. This may sound cynical until one reads the conference brochures that represent the current state of practice and that are attended by HRD specialists. They then go back to their organizations with the latest how-to's, which just happen to coincide with the latest books top management is reading. And then a year later they read in *Fortune* or *The Wall Street Journal* about the failure of the latest management approach to lead to organizational effectiveness.

The only way HRD can transition from this stage is to present interventions to our clients that have been developed from theory and research. We also need to convince our clients there are no magic answers to organizational effectiveness.

There Is Nothing More Practical Than a Good Theory

Although the field needs to generate and adapt theory, as well as conduct more research, we also need to heed Lewin's words in ensuring that theory and research gets translated into practice. Yet theory building and research is a relatively new and somewhat maligned activity outside of the HRD academic setting (Chalofsky and Reinhart, 1988). Practitioners do not have the time or incentive to read research-based articles, organizational HRD functions do not consider many of their data-gathering and inquiry-based studies as research, and many organizations will not share their research for proprietary reasons. In addition, practitioners do not have any incentive to publish research; academics do have incentive to publish, but in scholarly journals that are only read by other academics. Actually, the state of HRD research is at the point now where adult education research was approximately fifteen years ago, when Kidd (1981) listed a number of criticisms in a discussion of adult education research needs. He stated that too often research arises out of the needs and interests of the researcher rather than the needs of the field; we pay little attention to research from other countries; we look at problems in settings that are not easily generalizable; and our writing about research "is as stylized as an airline timetable, and only half as exciting" (p. 57).

The research being conducted needs to inform practice, the research findings need to get into the hands of the practitioners, and the practitioners need to be willing to apply the research findings in and with their client organizations. Merriam (1986) makes several suggestions to facilitate the research-to-practice transition. One is to find people who act as links between researchers and practitioners; in our field they could be the consultants and practitioners who are also graduate students. They need to read and conduct research for their studies and can help to translate and apply research findings. The Academy for HRD has instituted a special group consisting of practitioners who are interested in research and has invited them to give feedback to the Academy on research needs and to support the dissemination of research. Another suggestion is more collaborative arrangements between researchers and practitioners. It has long been the practice of consultants and their clients to make joint presentations at conferences; the same could be encouraged for researchers and their clients, especially where the relationship to practice is built into the research design, such as action research, case study research, and other forms of qualitative research. Making research results easily understood would help the transition. ASTD's *Training and Development* has a section that is included quarterly called "Research Capsules," and the Academy of Management's *Executive* has a section called "Research Translations." Both summarize research studies and gear the writing for practitioners.

Conclusion

There are now over two hundred academic programs in HRD and related fields. The research emanating from these programs has begun to have an effect on the field. In addition, the number of graduates in managerial and consulting positions must also be growing, given the number of graduates from all these programs. This will result in HRD professionals who appreciate research. Professional credibility will begin to be based on a theoretically sound body of knowledge, so HRD practice will be able to give clients what they truly need and will be valued and trusted as an authentic agent of organization change and effectiveness.

References

Bureau of Training. *An Outline of Learning Experiences for the Employee Development Specialist.* Washington, D.C.: U.S. Civil Service Commission, 1976.

Chalofsky, N. "What Is HRD?" In D. Gradous (ed.), *Systems Theory Applied to Human Resource Development.* Alexandria, Va.: American Society for Training and Development, 1989.

Chalofsky, N., and Lincoln, C. *Up the HRD Ladder.* Reading, Mass.: Addison-Wesley, 1983.

Chalofsky, N., and Reinhart, C. *Effective Human Resource Development.* San Francisco: Jossey-Bass, 1988.

Dixon, N., and Henkelman, J. *The Academic Guide: A Volume in Models for HRD Practice.* Alexandria, Va.: American Society for Training and Development, 1991.

Jacobs, R. "Human Resource Development as an Interdisciplinary Body of Knowledge." *Human Resource Development Quarterly,* 1990, 1 (1), 65–71.

Jarvis, P. (ed.). *Twentieth Century Thinkers in Adult Education.* London: Croom Helm, 1987.

Jensen, G. "How Adult Education Borrows and Reformulates Knowledge of Other Disciplines". In G. Jensen, A. Liveright, and W. Hallenback (eds.), *Adult Education: Outlines of an Emerging Field of University Study.* Washington, D.C.: Adult Education Association, 1964.

Kidd, J. R. "Educational Research Needs in Adult Education." *Convergence: An International Journal of Adult Education,* 1981, 14 (2), 53–62.

Lippitt, G., and Nadler, L. "Emerging Roles of the Training Director." *Training and Development,* 1967, 21 (8), 2–10.

Merriam, S. "The Research-to-Practice Dilemma." *Lifelong Learning: An Omnibus of Practice and Research,* 1986, 10 (1), 4–6, 24.

McLagan, P. *Models for Excellence.* Alexandria, Va.: American Society for Training and Development, 1983.

McLagan, P. *Models for HRD Practice.* Alexandria, Va.: American Society for Training and Development, 1989.

Nadler, L. *Developing Human Resources.* (3rd ed.) San Francisco: Jossey-Bass, 1990.

Watkins, K., and Willis, V. "Theoretical Foundations for the Models of HRD Practice: A Critique." In N. Dixon and J. Henkelman (eds.), *Academic Guide to the Models for HRD Practice.* Alexandria, Va.: American Society for Training and Development, 1991.

NEAL E. CHALOFSKY is associate professor and director of the human resource development program at George Washington University, Washington, D.C.

This chapter examines reflective theory building in practice as an appropriate role for the practitioner and a significant means of contributing to the knowledge base of adult education and human resource development.

Knowledge Comes from Practice: Reflective Theory Building in Practice

Vivian W. Mott

The dialogue goes something like this: researchers lament, If practitioners would only use the research that we put in front of them. To which practitioners respond, If only the findings were written so that someone other than researchers could understand and use them! Dialogues such as these echo the concerns of many researchers regarding the almost nonexistent use of theory among practitioners, concerns matched by practitioners in adult and continuing education and human resource development (HRD), who sadly point out that the research that might help is frequently written in *academese* and published in obscure, expensive, and largely inaccessible scholarly journals. These comments and others like them point, more basically, to a long-recognized need for a stronger, more positive relationship between research and practice.

Few would dispute the value of theory—not only as guidance for practice, but also as a means of promoting dialogue. But theories are not abstractions generated in a practical vacuum; theories are, or should be, born of inquiry and challenges in practice. And although practitioners may voice their distaste for formal theory, often finding it irrelevant, difficult to understand, and harder to apply, "there is plenty of evidence to show that . . . many practitioners devise their own patterns of practice (theories-in-use) and consciously infuse their activities with intuitive, artistic elements" (Brookfield, 1986, p. 246). What should follow, then, are the acknowledgment and support of practice-oriented research in which informal activities and patterns of practice become formalized and disseminated to others in one's field of practice.

The primary tenet of this chapter is that practitioners quite appropriately and effectively engage in reflective theory building, and in doing so, generate expert knowledge for use in practice. The chapter explores several factors that affect practice-oriented research: the tenuous and problematic relationship between research and practice (based predominantly in our positivist view of science), the changing nature of professional practice, and the concept of reflective practice as a necessary precursor to reflective theory building. Strategies that promote practice-based research are also considered. The goal of the chapter is to encourage less of a distinction between the act of research and the person at the heart of the inquiry and to show that the reflective practitioner can and should be both researcher and practitioner.

Relationship Between Theory and Practice

Many in the fields of adult and continuing education and HRD express concern about the relationship between research and practice (See, for example, Brookfield, 1986; Carr and Kemmis, 1986; Cervero, 1991; or Deshler and Hagan, 1989), and suggest that the tenuous relationship is primarily a manifestation of the positivist view of knowledge production. Although professionals may intuitively feel that research and practice should be closely related, there is a "great disparity between theory and practice, which frustrates those who consider themselves practitioners and concerns those who consider themselves theoreticians" (Cervero, 1991, p. 19). At the heart of the discord are beliefs about the nature and value of science itself, the purpose of research, and even who researchers should be.

According to the positivist paradigm, knowledge resides outside the individual; research and the production of knowledge are reserved for the scholar, and are incapable of being done well by the practitioner. Jenne even contends that questions about "who creates knowledge, for what purposes, as well as how knowledge is legitimized and what criteria should be used to judge its usefulness" (1994, p. 61) are really issues of control and power. He argues, for example, in regard to the dissemination of educational research, that "a hierarchy of journals exists that, in many respects, reflects the hierarchy about what counts as legitimate knowledge (for example, scholarly versus practice-generated)" (p.65). For purposes of this discussion, *Adult Education Quarterly, Educational Researcher,* and *HRD Quarterly* are among those at the top of the hierarchy, whereas others are considered less legitimate and scholarly. So, although practice-based research may have intuitive appeal, practitioners are confronted with consistent messages concerning the lack of legitimacy of practice-generated knowledge as well as philosophical and practical difficulty in generating scholarly information in environments that discourage active and collaborative inquiry. What results are the disenfranchisement of potential researchers, continued external control of the professions, and an unexamined reproduction of the status quo regarding the separation of theory and practice.

Practitioners in various fields have specifically addressed the complex and dynamic relationship between theory and practice. Murphy, for instance, identifies three related concepts—research, theory, and practice—as a triangle that she says represents the "insider world of adult education" (1992, p. 61).

According to Murphy, those in the triangle are frequently referred to as reflective practitioners and are vulnerable to "exploitation by the overly theory- or practice-oriented individuals within adult education. . . . The notion of the 'reflective practitioner' held 'captive' in the semi-Bermudan 'triangle' of adult education theory, research, and practice worries me even more. Not because it makes those caught in the triangle disappear but because it loses sight of those outside, or on the periphery of it" (p. 61).

In her continued metaphorical explanation, Murphy stresses that such a model "does not match the reality of adult education research in the changing research contexts" (1992, p. 61) nor the complexity of adult education, HRD, and other professional fields of the 1990s and beyond.

In a move toward professionalization, educators and others in social science fields have promoted a problematic dependence on science as well. Carl Rogers regarded science as beneficial only as long as it emerged out of and held meaning for his practice, and wrote of his discomfort with the "gap between these two roles" (1955, p. 267) of scientist and practitioner. In a similar vein, Peters and Waterman maintain that in trying to professionalize, we tend to forget that "good theory comes from inside the organization," and they suggest that HRD practitioners should conduct "skilled inquiry into the problems of everyday business" (1982, p. 183).

Ever-changing social structures, demands for professional accountability, quickened obsolescence of professional knowledge, and the changing nature of professional practice call for the immediate and contextual attention given by those engaged in practice, not solely that of the theorist. According to Brown and Elfenbein, practitioners "find themselves in an increasingly complex, changing environment where unique, new, or unusual cases are encountered and the models or theories generated in the scientific paradigm do not apply" (1991, p. 77). In response to this environment, they propose a model of inquiry that stresses the practitioner's ability to learn from practice in a contextual and reiterative way and then transfer that understanding into new knowledge that is both rigorous and relevant for practice.

This bridging of action and theory, of the concrete and abstract, was the central idea in Lewin's earlier work in action science (1948). Lewin was, according to Argyris (1993), a "pioneer researcher-intervener, [who] showed that [research] could be placed in the service of change" (p. 10). His research efforts focused on critical problems of the real world, such as democracy, nutrition, and economics, and his theories were immediately tested in the environments from which they were derived. Today, the Lewinian model of social science challenges the dominant positivist epistemology by proposing action research as a means of solving social problems through a reiterative process of diagnosis, action, and evaluation.

Reflective Theory Building in Professional Practice

Argyris and Schön fear, however, that the "ideal of a working relationship between research and practice has yet to be realized" (1974, pp. 3–4). They suggest a new epistemology of practice, one that assumes a reflective posture, both grounded in theory and actively engaged in the generation of new knowledge in the context of practice. Argyris and Schön maintain that "theories are theories regardless of their origin: there are practical, common-sense theories as well as academic or scientific theories . . . [that are] only a set of interconnected propositions . . . a vehicle for exploration" (pp. 4–5). And, according to Argyris and Schön, the informal but expert knowledge gained through such inquiry is a crucial dimension of expertise and a natural outcome of reflective thinking in practice.

According to Dewey, "*reflective* [original emphasis] thinking . . . involves (1) a state of doubt, hesitation, perplexity, mental difficulty, in which thinking originates, and (2) an act of searching, hunting, inquiring, to find material that will resolve the doubt, settle and dispose of the perplexity" (1933, p. 12). The entire process of reflection is aimed at the solution of the perplexity through the reiterative process of exploration, reflection, and renewed exploration in the midst of practice. In other words, reflective practice is the "capacity for thinking about . . . actions while engaged in the midst of practice. This active consideration of one's knowledge and behavior aids in reframing the challenges of practice, and enables the professional to cope more successfully with novelty and uncertainty of practice for a more appropriate response" (Mott, 1994, p. 12).

Reflection, as it is used in this context, is actually closer to what Schön (1983, 1988) refers to as *reflection-for-action,* that is, a combination of *reflection-on-action,* undertaken after the fact, and *reflection-in-action,* spontaneously occurring in the midst of action itself. With the prime goal of improving practice, reflection-for-action enables practitioners to determine the efficacy of their actions, and is a precursor to practice interventions, theories-in-use, or "adjustments-in-action" (Mott, 1994). It is in this state of reflection-for-action that inquiry and *reflective theory building* begin.

According to Schön, theories-in-use represent the synthesis of both formal and explicit theories, and the informal and incidental knowledge that guides the action of practitioners. In "unfamiliar situations when the problem is not initially clear and there is no obvious fit between the characteristics of the situation and the available body of theories" (1988, p. 34), theories-in-use are constructed by the practitioner to fill in the gaps and extend one's technical knowledge. Examples abound in every discipline of formal, academic knowledge emerging through the pursuit and articulation of informal knowledge gained in answer to the many challenges of practice—the reflection of an HRD director in search of an appropriate means of management or training, the literacy volunteer's scrutiny of applicable reading materials, or the educator's quest for the most relevant examples for a critical point of understanding. This critical and reflective inquiry into problematic aspects of daily practice involves reflective problem setting, framing or reframing the situation in terms of a specific context, conscious examination of the unfamiliar or problematic circumstance, and the articulating and formalizing one's theories-in-use. The goal, according to Schön, is the thoughtful integration of formal theory, reflection, and practical knowledge and expertise. This, then, is the process of *reflective theory building* in which the reflective practitioner consciously reflects on the challenges of practice, reiteratively engages in problem posing, data gathering, action, evaluation, and reflection, and then shares the knowledge produced with others in practice.

Promotion of Practice-Based Research

An important element in the promotion and use of reflective theory building is, of course, a sufficient level of expertise, one of firmly understanding and reflectively applying the tenets of one's practice, "only then to develop and test new forms of understanding and action where familiar categories and ways of thinking fail" (Schön, 1988, p. 40). Schön and others refer to a crisis of confidence where professional practice is concerned, a crisis tied inexorably to academic preparation and the nature and quality of professional knowledge in light of the ever-changing needs and critical problems of society. All too often, professional schools, for instance, privilege scientific knowledge and technical rationality, resulting in an epistemology of practice ill-suited for today's changing workplace. Educators in many disciplines, however, recognize the value of education and training in applied research activities, and share the belief that the promotion of practice-based research results in improved practice strategies, professional growth, and greater professional identification and ownership. According to scholars-practitioners in educational administration (Achilles, 1989; Osterman and Kottkamp, 1993), human resource development (Brown and Elfenbein, 1991; Peters and Waterman, 1982; Watkins and Marsick, 1993), and various adult educational practices (Beaudoin, 1991), inquiry and investigation in the service of addressing challenges in classrooms, laboratories, and other practice environments are inherent in reflective practice. Graduate and postgraduate education in research methodologies are considered crucial for continued professional development and instructional improvement and are a mechanism for creating change in response to societal demands.

It isn't only students who are resistant or even antagonistic toward research, however. Many faculty, administrators, clinicians, and others simply do not consider themselves researchers, and few produce or even read research. Although actively engaged in practice-based research in an informal manner, some feel insufficiently trained, and therefore unprepared to conduct and share research that might improve practice. Among the several reasons for this estrangement are a perceived lack of practical relevance in the research being conducted, inadequate graduate training and experience in research methodologies, work environments that are not conducive to research, and communication failure among traditional researchers and practitioners. At the core of these issues is a basic values conflict between the philosophical orientations of many practitioners and the underlying assumptions regarding traditional research, the nature of reality, and knowledge production.

Many of the concerns about inadequate preparation for conducting research in practice could be addressed by involving students in research education and practice early in their professional preparation programs. But what of those already in practice without the opportunity for formal research training? In practice settings with an emphasis on production, pressure to follow established routines, and little time for reflection, administrators and educators must strive to provide atmospheres supportive of reflection, inquiry, and theory building. Through the practical application of research skills in classrooms, clinical settings, and boardrooms, and through mentoring programs that encourage positive attitudes toward practice-based research, new and experienced practitioners would be more likely to perceive themselves as reflective, theory-building practitioners whose effective professional strategies include and promote practical, self-generated knowledge as well as formal theory.

Conclusion

Unfortunately, the schism that exists between practice and theory has the potential to weaken both, resulting in a lack of appreciation of the problems in practice, continued research of irrelevant issues, and diminished use of research by practitioners, not to mention the potential unreflective application of research findings to critical problems of practice. Resolution lies partly in the continued acceptance of alternative research paradigms and a broadened philosophy of science that values reflective theory building as a complementary and equally constructive path to knowledge production. Reflective theory building is really a matter of bringing about and managing change. Watkins and Marsick maintain that whether in adult and continuing education, clinical practice, or human resource development, "change is a cyclical process of creating knowledge . . . disseminating it, implementing the change, and then institutionalizing what is learned" (1993, p. 21). Given the complex, dynamic, and challenging times of change in all professional fields of practice, expert knowledge must be generated by those who are not only capable, but who have a vested interest in the process and product. Those persons are reflective practitioners rightly engaged in reflective theory building.

References

Achilles, C. M. "The Practice of Research on Practice." Paper presented at the annual meeting of the University Council on Educational Administration, Scottsdale, Arizona, October 1989. (ED 325 902)

Argyris, C. Knowledge for Action: A Guide to Overcoming Barriers to Organizational Change. San Francisco: Jossey-Bass, 1993.

Argyris, C., and Schön, D. A. Theory in Practice: Increasing Professional Effectiveness. San Francisco: Jossey-Bass, 1974.

Beaudoin, M. F. "Researching Practice and Practicing Research. A Critique of Distance Education Research and Writing." Paper presented at the 11th national conference on Alternative and External Degree Programs for Adults, Mobile, Alabama, October 1991.

Brookfield, S. D. *Understanding and Facilitating Adult Learning: A Comprehensive Analysis of Principles and Effective Practices*. San Francisco: Jossey-Bass, 1986.

Brown, S. M., and Elfenbein, M. H. "Experiential Learning: Reflection on Practice and the Organizational Action Scientist." Paper presented at the 11th national conference on Alternative and External Degree Programs for Adults, Mobile, Alabama, October 1991.

Carr, W., and Kemmis, S. *Becoming Critical: Education, Knowledge, and Action Research*. London: Falmer Press, 1986.

Cervero, R. M. "Changing Relationship Between Theory and Practice." In J. M. Peters, P. Jarvis, and Associates (eds.), *Adult Education: Evolution and Achievements in a Developing Field of Study*. San Francisco: Jossey-Bass, 1991.

Deshler, D., and Hagan, N. "Adult Education Research: Issues and Directions." In S. B. Merriam and P. M. Cunningham (eds.), *Handbook of Adult and Continuing Education*. San Francisco: Jossey-Bass, 1989.

Dewey, J. *How We Think: A Restatement of the Relation of Reflective Thinking to the Educative Process*. Boston: D.C. Heath, 1933.

Jenne, J. T. "Why Teacher Research?" In E. W. Ross (ed.), *Reflective Practice in Social Studies*. Washington, D.C.: National Council for the Social Studies, Bulletin No. 88, 1994. (ED 373 014)

Lewin, K. "Action Research and Minority Problems." In G. W. Lewin (ed.), *Resolving Social Conflicts*. New York: Harper, 1948.

Mott, V. W. "A Phenomenological Inquiry Into the Role of Intuition in Reflective Adult Education Practice." Unpublished doctoral dissertation, Department of Adult Education, University of Georgia, 1994.

Murphy, B. "Adult Education and the Changing Research Context." In N. Miller and L. West (eds.), *Proceedings of the 22nd Annual SCUTREA Conference*. Canterbury, UK, July 1992. (ED 358 290)

Osterman, K. F., and Kottkamp, R. B. *Reflective Practice for Educators: Improving Schooling Through Professional Development*. Newbury Park, Calif.: Corwin Press, 1993.

Peters, T. J., and Waterman, R. H. *In Search of Excellence: Lessons From America's Best-run Companies*. New York: Warner Books, 1982.

Rogers, C. R. "Persons or Science? A Philosophical Question." *American Psychologist*, 1955, 10, 267–278.

Schön, D. A. *The Reflective Practitioner*. San Francisco: Jossey-Bass, 1983.

Schön, D. A. *Educating the Reflective Practitioner*. San Francisco: Jossey-Bass, 1988.

Watkins, K. E., and Marsick, V. J. *Sculpting the Learning Organization: Lessons in the Art and Science of Systematic Change*. San Francisco: Jossey-Bass, 1993.

VIVIAN W. MOTT is assistant professor of adult education at East Carolina University in Greenville, North Carolina, and president of Wilson Mott & Associates, a consulting, training, and human resource development firm.

PART FOUR

Should Practitioners Educating Adults in the Workplace Be Credentialed?

There are compelling reasons why people who are involved in facilitating workplace learning should resist efforts toward professional licensing.

Human Resource Development Practitioners Should Resist Professional Licensing

Jerry W. Gilley

In the early 1950s, human resource development (HRD) practitioners began examining their respective roles and ways of improving the professionalized status of the field. As recounted in the *Professional Standards Committee Report of Activity* (American Society for Training and Development, 1953), the issue of professional credentialing for the field was being examined as a means of advancing the field. The committee reported that "after considering the matter at some length the conclusion was reached that this is not the appropriate time to deal with the question of certification. . . . Since considerations cannot be delayed indefinitely if training is to establish itself as a real profession, it may be desirable to make a thorough study of the entire matter as a basis for future action by the American Society for Training Directors" (Gilley and Eggland, 1989, p.309).

Today, occupational classifications include professions, semiprofessions, paraprofessions, quasiprofessions, and skilled and unskilled professions. What separates occupational classifications are the level of knowledge or competencies requirement, level of importance to society, and level of control by members of the occupation (Galbraith and Sisco, 1992; Gilley and Galbraith, 1987). Therefore, occupations can be evaluated on the basis of their importance and the difficulty of the tasks that are associated with them. Consequently, occupational classifications are not based on the service itself, but on the nature of service. By determining the nature of service, society can classify an occupation (Gilley and Eggland, 1989). This helps society separate one occupation from another and develop an orientation to various occupations.

However, it is difficult to define what makes a professional and what constitutes a profession to everyone's satisfaction. Bullett (1981) defined a profession as a "field of human endeavor with a well-defined body of knowledge, containing basic principles common to all applications and techniques unique to the field, with practitioners skilled and experienced in applying these techniques, and dedicated to the public interest" (p. 5). Each of these elements can be used as a standard by which occupational fields are measured. These elements are also the foundation of the professionalization process.

Purposes of Professional Licensure

The primary purpose of professional licensure is "to protect the public from incompetent practitioners" (Miller 1976, p. 6). Such programs help guarantee that the public is kept safe from malpractice.

Although professional licensure holds as its principal purpose the protection of the public from incompetent practitioners, other purposes have been identified. They include promoting professionalism and enhancing the prestige of the profession through the improvement of its public image and protecting employers by providing them a means of comparing potential applicants. These purposes are accomplished through the identification and development of a body of knowledge, a set of competencies, and a regulatory mechanism that evaluates the proficiency of practitioners before they can achieve professional status (Gilley, 1986). Such efforts communicate to the public the deep concerns that the profession has regarding the quality of its members.

Because a profession recognizes only licensed practitioners, a restriction on the number of qualified persons entering the profession is maintained, creating a sense of continuity. In addition, HRD practitioners who are licensed may have increased job security. Therefore, an indirect result of the professional licensure process is that it encourages HRD practitioners to remain in their chosen profession.

Negative Implications of Professional Licensure

Regardless of the benefits of professional licensure, the following negative implications must be considered by HRD practitioners.

Regulation of the Field. Professional licensure is a gatekeeping activity for a profession. The entry of qualified individuals is severely limited, which increases the responsibility of existing practitioners to carry out the mission set forth by HRD. However, the quality of the profession may not be improved as a result of restricting entry of practitioners (Mager and Cram, 1985).

Because of the diversity, complexity, and size of the field of HRD, it is incorrect to assume that HRD-related associations and societies are in a position to regulate and control the profession. To date, no single association or society can adequately regulate or control the profession. Therefore, restricting entry through professional licensure is not a viable option.

Diversity and Complexity. The field of HRD is diverse and interdisciplinary in nature, and although attempts have been made to identify a set of standards, outputs, and competencies for the field of HRD (Manager Competencies in 1991; Models for HRD Practice in 1989; Instructors' Competencies in 1988), their acceptance and application has not been universal. Without an agreed-on set of competencies, a professional licensure program would certainly fragment the field of HRD and its practitioners into powerless and ineffective camps designed to protect their special interests.

Divisiveness. The divisiveness of a professional licensure program is obvious. The topic immediately forces HRD practitioners to draw battle lines: those for professional licensure versus those against it. Rather than discussing the many ways HRD can improve organizational effectiveness, HRD practitioners argue about professional licensure. Such arguments can distract practitioners from their goals. In addition, many HRD practitioners are threatened by a restrictive process such as professional licensure.

Evaluation Procedures. One of the major obstacles in creating a professional licensure program is determining who in the profession is able to establish measurable standards by which to evaluate HRD practitioners. In addition, selecting appropriate and comprehensive qualification criteria can be a demanding task. The question of what form or forms should be used to test and measure the competence of HRD practitioners is very complicated. For example, should experience be used as a criterion and, if so, should it be based on length of experience, type of experience, or both? Should a detailed portfolio be used as a qualification criterion, or should interviews, paper and pencil tests, performance evaluations, or client referrals also be a part of the assessment? In selecting the appropriate criteria, an awareness of the validity and reliability of such measurements is needed, as well as a cognizance of the diversity and complexity of HRD. Presently, few, if any, HRD practitioners possess such a holistic awareness.

Lack of Need. The principal argument for professional licensure is that it protects the public from incompetent practitioners. However, is the public at risk from poor instructors, or inadequate instructional designers, or incompetent HRD consultants or managers? The answer is no. That being the case, what is the public being protected from (Mager and Cram, 1985)? The answer is nothing. In addition, HRD practitioners working in the corporate or industrial arenas do not provide service to the public. In fact, corporate clients are quite capable of protecting themselves from incompetent HRD practitioners and do so often. Professional licensure is a process that can only divide the field and add unnecessary complexity to the lives of its practitioners. It cannot enhance the image of the field or improve the quality of professional service (Sork and Welock, 1992).

Professionalization Process

Many believe that the professionalization process consists of formal activities such as certification, accreditation, and licensure (Gilley, Geis, and Seyfer,

1987; Gilley and Galbraith, 1986; Bratton and Hildebrand, 1980). Such activities can help define an occupation and the competencies required by its practitioners but are not prescriptive for each and every occupational field. However, professionalizing a field is more complex than simply implementing a credentialing process. It is an organized and systematic approach designed to bring an occupation to a higher level of status (Collins, 1992). According to Gilley and Galbraith (1987), "professionalization of an occupational field can be examined from four perspectives: a philosophical orientation, a developmental orientation that is comprised of various stages, a characteristics orientation, and a nontraditional approach" (p. 97). Each of these perspectives is used to provide evidence regarding the professionalized nature of HRD as well as to determine the feasibility of professional licensure for HRD practitioners.

Philosophical Orientation. The philosophical orientation to professionalization is based on individuals' attitudes, their sense of calling, and their perspectives on personal freedom, public service, and self-regulation. Each of these determines the level of professionalization required of an occupational field.

Because of the diverse nature of many fields, it is impossible to establish a single process by which practitioners can achieve ideal professionalized status. The advent of an accepted set of competencies, outputs, and standards, such as identified in the *Models for HRD Practice* (1989), can provide the foundation for such a process to be established (Gilley and Galbraith, 1986).

Developmental Orientation. Many believe that a profession evolves through various stages in order to achieve optimal professionalized status (Whyte, 1977). The developmental process begins with an informal association of interested individuals who maintain a common occupational interest. Identifying and adopting a distinct body of knowledge is the second stage. Formally organizing practitioners into an institute or society as a means of exchanging ideas, techniques, and knowledge is the third stage. Identifying entry requirements, based either on experience alone or on a combination of experience and qualifications, is the fourth stage. Establishing ethical and disciplinary codes is the fifth stage. The final stage of the developmental process of professionalization is revising of entry requirements, through which academic qualifications and a specific period of experience become mandatory for practitioners.

The field of HRD has, however, failed to progress systematically through all six developmental stages. Some stages have been accomplished; for example, the field has several professional societies that enable its practitioners to exchange ideas, knowledge, and techniques. Some work has been done in establishing a standardized body of knowledge, but establishing entry requirement for HRD practitioners, identifying and utilizing ethical and disciplinary codes, and mandating academic and work experience standards have not been fully developed.

Characteristic Orientation. Vollmer and Mills (1966) reported three decades ago that several specific characteristics assist in the evolutionary process toward professional status. According to this orientation, each of the characteristics must be in place and fully developed before a discipline is considered a profession (Gilley and Eggland, 1989).

According to Scheer (1964), a profession contains eight essential and interrelated characteristics, which are vital in its development. However, the importance placed on different characteristics varies from occupation to occupation. The eight characteristics include

1. A code of ethics
2. An organized and accepted body of knowledge
3. Specialized skills or identified competencies
4. A minimum education requirement
5. Proficiency testing
6. A process ensuring that members fulfill their responsibilities
7. Promulgation and exchange of ideas among members
8. Enforcement of the disciplines of the profession

In the field of HRD, the opportunity for the exchange of ideas (the seventh characteristic) is the only characteristic that clearly applies. A code of ethics (the first characteristic) is present in the membership documents of all major HRD societies; for example, the Society for Human Resource Management (SHRM), the American Society for Training Performance and Instruction (ASTPI), and the International Society of Performance and Instruction (ISPI). However, the enforcement of a code of ethics is quite rare.

The establishment of an accepted body of knowledge (the second characteristic) and the identification of specialized skills or competencies (the third characteristic) have received considerable attention during the past several years in HRD-related societies. In a 1983 study, *Models for Excellence,* a comprehensive list of thirty-one competencies and the fifteen roles of training and development professionals were identified. In 1989, the *Models for HRD Practice* (McLagan and Suhadolnik), a revised version of the *Models for Excellence,* was published. The focus was expanded to include roles and competencies of HRD practitioners, and one additional area, that of career development, was included. The major contribution of this study, however, was the identification of outputs and standards for each HRD role.

In another development, a nonprofit organization specializing in competency research, the International Board of Standards for Training, Performance, and Instruction (IBSTPI), was established in 1985. During the past decade, IBSTPI published competency studies for instructional designers, instructors, and HRD managers.

Regardless of the efforts in the past, a universally accepted body of knowledge and set of skills and competencies still does not exist. It would be inappropriate to create a professional licensure program until these critical issues have been decided.

There is no certifying body that tests the proficiency of HRD practitioners (the fifth characteristic). The Society of Human Resource Management (SHRM) does provide certification of its members through a joint venture with the Personnel Accreditation Institute (PAI). Today, the PAI offers certification on two levels: Professional in Human Resources (PHR) and Senior Professional in Human Resources (SPHR). The American Compensation Association (ACA) offers certification for compensation practitioners on completion of a course of study. However, neither SHRM nor ACA represents the majority of the practitioners in the field of HRD. The International Society for Performance and Instruction (ISPI) and the American Society for Training and Development (ASTD) have failed to endorse a credentialing process for their members. Thus, the field of HRD clearly fails to exhibit the fifth characteristic of a profession.

Finally, the field of HRD is so loosely organized that it does not maintain an orderly process to ensure the fulfillment of professional responsibilities (the sixth characteristic), nor does it demand that its practitioners accept the discipline of other professionals for malpractice or unprofessional behavior (the eighth characteristic) or maintain a minimum education requirement for its practitioners (the fourth characteristic). As a result, HRD practitioners can perform any way they see fit regardless of the effect that their behavior has on the field.

Nontraditional Orientation. Another view of professionalization is that the individuals who belong to an occupational group should determine the tenets of their profession (Cervero, 1985). According to Galbraith and Gilley (1987), "The nontraditional perspective maintains that the members of a discipline are able to discern the unique characteristics and needs of the occupation. Because of this awareness, they are better able to identify the essential elements that constitute what they believe to be a profession" (p. 17). The nontraditional approach to professionalization seriously questions the need for professional licensure or any other credentialing process because they cannot adequately measure the diverse dimensions that encompass a specific occupation. Given the diversity of the field of HRD, Mager and Cram (1985) believe the nontraditional orientation has significant merit. Practitioners who embrace it may select any and all of the components identified by other professionalization orientations. In other words, the nontraditional orientation allows HRD practitioners the freedom to accept the components they believe are essential in the development of their professional identities.

Conclusion

Some HRD practitioners believe that professional licensure will help improve the professionalization of HRD (Lee, 1986). However, this approach is less than acceptable because it employs a formal regulatory approach to professionalization that most practitioners do not desire (Sork and Welock, 1992; Gilley, 1986; Mager and Cram, 1985).

A less formal approach, one that emphasizes individual freedom, democratic peer review, and the free market system, as opposed to the development of a systematic process requiring each member of an occupation to acquire the official body of knowledge, appears to be more appropriate for the field of HRD (Mager and Cram, 1985). Such an approach would not view professional licensure as a viable process for advancing the field because of its controlling and restrictive nature. A less formal approach accepts the tenets of self-regulation and control, which can include continuing professional development as well as other forms of professional development.

Each of the four perspectives of professionalization maintains that professionalized status can be obtained by an occupational field. They differ, however, in their approach, requirements, degree of formality, and measurement techniques. Although three of these four orientations (the philosophical, developmental, and characteristic) allow professional licensure as a means of enhancing professionalization, five barriers prevent the implementation of professional licensure for the field of HRD. They include (1) the wide diversity, complexity, and size of the field, (2) the lack of practitioner control demonstrated by HRD-related societies, (3) the inadequacy of testing and evaluation procedures, (4) the lack of a real need of professional licensure, and (5) the loosely organized nature of the field. Any of these barriers is sufficient to prevent the implementation of a professional licensure program for the field of HRD.

References

American Society for Training and Development. *Professional Standards Committee Report of Activity*. Madison, Wis.: American Society for Training and Development, 1953.

Bratton, B., and Hildebrand, M. "Plain Talk About Professional Certification." *Instructional Innovator*, 1980, 25 (9), 22–24, 49.

Bullett, F. "Why Certification?" *Certification Registration and Information*. Washington, D.C.: American Production and Inventory Society, 1981.

Cervero, R. M. "The Predicament of Professionalism for Adult Education." *Adult Literacy and Basic Education*, 1985, 9 (1), 11–17.

Collins, M. "Adult and Continuing Education Should Strive for Professionalization." In M. W. Galbraith and B. R. Sisco (eds.), *Confronting Controversies in Challenging Times: A Call for Action*. New Directions for Adult and Continuing Education, no. 54. San Francisco: Jossey-Bass, 1992.

Galbraith, M. W., and Gilley, J. W. *Professional Certification: Implications for Adult Education and HRD*. Columbus, Ohio: National Center for Research in Adult, Career, and Vocational Education, 1987.

Galbraith, M. W., and Sisco, B. R. (eds.). *Confronting Controversies in Challenging Times: A Call for Action*. New Directions for Adult and Continuing Education, no. 54. San Francisco: Jossey-Bass, 1992.

Gilley, J. W. "The Characteristics and Developmental Stages of a Profession: Does HRD Measure Up?" *Personnel Administrator*, 1986, 40 (1), 14–18.

Gilley, J. W., and Eggland, S. A. *Principles of Human Resource Development*. Reading, Mass.: Addison-Wesley, 1989.

Gilley, J. W., and Galbraith, M. W. "Examining Professional Certification." *Training and Development*, 1986, 40 (6), 60–61.

Gilley, J. W., and Galbraith, M. W. "Professionalization and Professional Certification: A Relationship." *Adult Education Research Conference Proceeding*. Laramie: University of Wyoming, 1987.

Gilley, J. W., Geis, G., and Seyfer, C. "Let's Talk Certification! Questions and Answers for the Profession About the Profession." *Performance Instruction*, 1987, 26 (1), 7–17.

International Board of Standards for Training, Performance, and Instruction. *Instructor Competencies: The Standards.* Vol. 1. Washington, D.C.: International Board of Standards for Training, Performance, and Instruction, 1988.

International Board of Standards for Training, Performance, and Instruction. *Manager Competencies.* Washington, D.C.: International Board of Standards for Training, Performance, and Instruction, 1991.

Lee, C. "Certification for Trainers: Thumbs Up." *Training and Development,* 1986, *23* (11), 54–64.

Mager, R. F., and Cram, D. D. "The Regulators Are Coming." *Training,* 1985, *21* (9), 40–45.

McLagan, P. A., and Bedrick, R. *Models for Excellence.* Alexandria, Va.: American Society for Training and Development, 1983.

McLagan, P. A., and Suhadolnik, D. *Models for HRD Practice.* Alexandria, Va.: American Society for Training and Development, 1989.

Miller, E. L. "Professionalism and Its Impact on Accreditation-type Programs." Paper presented to the American Society of Personnel Administrators, Washington, D.C., 1976.

Scheer, W. E. "Is Personnel Management a Profession?" *Personnel,* 1964, *43* (5), 225–261.

Sork, T. J., and Welock, B. A. "Professional Certification Is Not Needed in Adult and Continuing Education." In M. W. Galbraith and B. R. Sisco, *Confronting Controversies in Challenging Times: A Call for Action.* New Directions for Adult and Continuing Education, no. 54. San Francisco: Jossey-Bass, 1992.

Vollmer, H., and Mills, D. *Professionalization.* Englewood Cliffs, N.J.: Prentice-Hall, 1966.

Whyte, G. S. "The Professional Practitioners in the Years to Come." Paper presented at the Institute of Personnel Management 21st conference, Washington, D.C., April 1977.

JERRY W. GILLEY is associate professor of Human Resource Development at Western Michigan University.

This chapter provides a brief overview of certification terminology, examines the growth of certification programs, and explores emerging issues that offer compelling reasons for training and human resource development practitioners to pursue certification in the workplace.

Human Resource Development Practitioners Should Strive for Certification

Andrea D. Ellinger

We live in a credentialed society. As consumers, we have come to expect that our physicians, nurses, dentists, dental hygienists, cosmetologists, attorneys, accountants, underwriters, and financial planners are competent in their professional practice. Although licensure, certification, and continuing professional education do not guarantee competence, they do establish acceptable standards of practice.

In the past twenty-five years, the fields of purchasing, materials management, and logistics have witnessed the continued development and refinement of a variety of professional certification programs (Wilkinson, 1992). The issue of certification has even been contemplated in the marketing field (Parmerlee, 1991). More recently, the computer industry has experienced a growth in certification programs; vendors such as Novell and Microsoft have established certification programs for their customers. In fact, since 1987, sixty thousand individuals have passed the CNE (certified Novell engineer) test, and fifty thousand have graduated as CNAs (certified Novell administrators) (Filipczak, 1995a). In addition to the certification offered to their customers, Microsoft, Novell, and the Educational Testing Service (ETS) have recently attempted to establish a certified technical trainer (CTT) standard (Filipczak, 1995b). Although Wiley (1992a) has acknowledged that the general public is not usually a direct consumer of the human resource manager's services, she has suggested that the public is often affected by policy decisions and recommendations made by human resource professionals. With the increasing complexities of the workplace, highly trained human resource professionals will be required as corporations recognize the strategic importance of their human resources.

Certification of adult educators, trainers, and human resource development (HRD) practitioners has been an issue that has been examined and debated in the field of adult education periodically over the years (Booth, 1984; Coscarelli, 1984; Galbraith and Gilley, 1985, 1987; James, 1992; White, 1992). This issue has also been discussed in the context of professionalization (Cervero, 1992; Collins, 1992). The growth of vendor certification programs and professional-association- and university-sponsored certificate and certification programs in the last decade (Holt, 1991; Lopos, 1991; Wiley, 1995), coupled with the dramatic changes occurring in the business environment, offers a compelling reason to reexamine the issue of certification of human resource professionals.

This chapter distinguishes between the definitional terms often associated with credentialing, reviews the recent literature on this topic, and explores emerging trends in the workplace affecting human resource professionals and certification. Finally, some of the arguments in support of certification for HRD practitioners are discussed.

Credentialing Terminology

Several terms associated with credentialing are often used interchangeably; however, researchers consider them to be distinct (Bratton and Hildebrand, 1980; Galbraith and Gilley, 1985). According to Galbraith and Gilley, professional certification is "a voluntary process by which a professional association or organization measures the competencies of individual practitioners" (1985, p. 12). Lee (1986), however, has defined certification more generally as the process of publicly attesting that a specified quality has been achieved or exceeded.

Although it becomes apparent that multiple definitions exist for certification, it should be distinguished from licensure and accreditation. Licensure is a mandatory legal requirement for certain professions that offers the public protection from incompetent practitioners. Licensure is similar to certification in that the recipient of either credential is an individual. Alternatively, accreditation is typically awarded to an institution rather than an individual. Bratton and Hildebrand (1980, p. 22) define accreditation as "the process whereby an agency or association grants public recognition to a school, college, or university, or specialized study program that meets certain predetermined qualifications or standards."

In addition, there is an important distinction between qualification and certification. Qualification refers to "the formal training process, developed using acceptable systematic methods, which prepares individuals to assume duties in a specified occupation (Lapp, 1992, p. 5), whereas certification is "the formal (and sometimes informal) evaluation process that determines, validates, and attests that individuals meet the technical competencies and skills that are prescribed for performing a specific occupation" (p. 6). Lapp contends that qualification is often the precursor to certification.

Another distinction should be made between certificate and certification programs. Holt (1991) acknowledges that the completion of a certificate program means the acquisition of certain proficiencies in concentrated areas of study. Settle (1991) suggests that a certificate is a document with a diploma-like format that is given to participants at the conclusion of a training experience to acknowledge their attendance. Certification programs, in contrast, tend to denote the measurement of competencies. However, a certificate-like document is typically provided to acknowledge certification and the completion of a certification program.

Growth of Certificate and Certification Programs

Certificate and certification programs are not new inventions (Lopos, 1991). Their growth has been influenced by expansion in areas of employment, by legislation continuously seeking to upgrade professional credentials, by advances in technology, and by the shift toward a global economy. A brief review of recent literature on certificate and certification programs in the human resources field is presented.

Certification in the Human Resource Management Field. Unlike the field of adult education, of which human resource development is considered a subfield by many, the human resource management field has four professional associations that provide certification. These are the Human Resource Certification Institute (HRCI), the American Compensation Association (ACA), the International Foundation of Employee Benefit Plans (IFEBP), and the Board of Certified Safety Professionals (BCSP) (Wiley, 1992a, 1995). The two certification designations awarded by the HRCI are the Professional in Human Resources (PHR) and the Senior Professional in Human Resources (SPHR); these are the only designations available for the human resource management field in general. The other associations award designations that represent specialized areas of human resources. Since its inception as the American Society for Personnel Administration Accreditation Institute (AAI) in 1975, the renamed HRCI has certified more than fourteen thousand HR professionals, and the number of candidates has increased from 150 in 1976 to 595 in 1986 to 2,052 in 1990 to nearly 4,000 in 1993 (Cherrington and Leonard, 1993; Wiley, 1992b). The increasing number of people sitting for the exams clearly demonstrates a strong interest in certification.

Certification in Training and Human Resource Development. Certification in human resource development and training and development (HRTD) has been pursued on two fronts (Smith, 1994). Professional associations constitute one front, and higher education the other front. Smith further subdivides certification in higher education into two categories: traditional and nontraditional paths. The traditional path includes formal degree programs at multiple levels ranging from the baccalaureate to the doctorate, whereas the nontraditional path includes continuing education units or proficiency certification that may or may not offer degree credit. Although professional associations have been in the forefront of the certification movement, they have been unsuccessful in their efforts to bring about professional certification. Conversely, higher education has been involved in certification efforts because traditional degree programs have been a major source of voluntary certification for years (Smith, 1994).

Smith's (1994) survey of the 1991 and 1993 American Society for Training and Development (ASTD) Academic Directories identified twenty-four nondegree certificate programs that appeared to specifically focus on human resource training and development (HRTD). Nineteen of the twenty-four programs were included in Smith's study, and of these, thirteen were identified as certificate programs, three as certification programs, and three as other. The annual program enrollment for these programs ranged from five to two hundred participants, and the programs had been in existence from one year to nineteen years. Three of these programs had formal relationships with local ASTD or National Society for Performance and Instruction (NSPI) chapters, and many had informal relationships with these organizations.

Nondegree Certificate Programs in HRD. Gaudet and Kotrlik (1995) conducted a study that was designed to describe HRD certificate programs currently offered by educational institutions throughout the United States and to determine the factors that are perceived by HRD certificate program administrators as influencing the development of such programs. Their findings suggest that sixteen primary factors serve as the foundation for the development of HRD certificate programs. The four factors perceived by program administrators as having the most effect on the development of these programs included changed work environments, career development, certificate programs' clientele, and the quality of the training professional. These findings also suggest that nondegree HRD certificate programs can, and do, play a role in the academic preparation of HRD practitioners (Gaudet and Kotrlik, 1995).

Trends in the Workplace Influencing Certification

There are several trends emerging in the workplace and in academia that have the potential to influence the certificate and certification program movement in the field of human resources. *Human resources* is the umbrella term that has been selected, because certificate and certification programs in training and human resource development and human resource management have been in existence for a number of years (Holt, 1991; Smith, 1994; Wiley, 1992a, 1992b, 1995). However, there is no formal, standardized certification process in the country associated with training and human resource development like the four previously mentioned professional associations in the human resource management discipline (Lapides, 1991). A standard certification for HRD certificate programs is also nonexistent (Gaudet and Kotrlik, 1995).

The workplace has become a complex and competitive environment. The proliferation of technology and the demands of the global economy are forcing many organizations to become increasingly reliant on knowledge creation and dissemination for sustained competitiveness. Because products and services can be easily replicated and reproduced, it has been argued that the rate at which individuals and organizations learn may become the only source of sustainable competitive advantage (Nonaka, 1991; Stata, 1989; Watkins and Marsick, 1993). This increased emphasis on learning at the individual, team, and organizational levels will affect the skills and competencies required of adult educators, trainers, and human resource professionals, particularly in organizations that espouse a learning philosophy. The traditional roles of trainers and human resource management and development practitioners will evolve, and new roles that call for a new set of skills and competencies will emerge (McLagan, 1996; Ulrich, Brockbank, Yeung, and Lake, 1995; Watkins, 1995). How will human resource professionals prepare for such changes and challenges? Certificate and certification programs offer promising solutions.

A Contingent Workforce. Many scholars have acknowledged that America has entered the age of the contingent or temporary worker, of the consultant and subcontractor, of the just-in-time workforce—fluid, flexible, and disposable (Morrow, 1993). The workers of the future will have to constantly sell their skills and reinvent their relationships with employers. Job security, according to Bridges (1994), resides in the person's employability, vendor-mindedness, and resiliency. He maintains that all jobs in today's economy are temporary, and that we have entered the age of a jobless society. Handy's (1990) vision of the organization is similar. He acknowledges that less than half the workforce in the industrial world will be holding conventional full-time jobs in organizations by the beginning of the twenty-first century. His depiction of the organizational structure is a shamrock, a three-leafed clover. The first leaf represents the essential core of the organization composed of professionals, technicians, and managers. The next two leaves are represented by contractors and temporary and part-time workers, respectively. The concepts of shamrock organization and the jobless society present a clear image of the workplace of the future. Employability will become dependent on a person's drive to update his or her credentials, acquire new skills, and remain knowledgeable about changes occurring in his or her respective field. A commitment to lifelong learning will be the only way to remain competitive in this changing job market. A survey of HRD executives conducted by ASTD ("Trends That Will Influence Workplace Learning . . .", 1994) also suggests that self-directed careers will become the norm, and that employees will have to assume more responsibility for their behaviors and learning.

Outsourcing. Investments in training and workplace education continue to increase, suggesting that training is a growing enterprise (Carnevale and Carnevale, 1994). A survey of annual training expenditures by the Lakewood Research Group reported that $52.2 billion had been spent by large organizations for training in 1995 ("1995 Industry Report"). This figure represents an estimated 1.59 billion hours of training for 49.6 million people. In addition, expenditures for outside sources of training increased by 4 percent between

1994 and 1995 to $10.3 billion, which represents 20 percent of total training expenditures. Further, 25 percent of organizations indicated that they are increasing their use of outsourcing as a business strategy.

Universal Performance Standards. The American Society for Training and Development's research ("Trends That Will Influence Workplace Learning . . . ," 1994) on business trends for learning professionals reveals that HRD executives' perceived universal performance standards will continue to increase. Such standards, modeled on the Malcolm Baldrige National Quality Award criteria and ISO 9000, will increase in use and importance. According to Filipczak (1995a), corporate training departments can now be formally certified by an independent agency as meeting certain standards of quality. Organizations can also seek certification for the processes by which they train and qualify their instructors. Given the endorsement of a set of criteria to be used for certifying the competence and professionalism of training departments by the International Board of Standards for Training, Performance, and Instruction (IBSTPI), is it unrealistic to expect that future certification standards could be developed for professional trainers?

Diverse Backgrounds of HR Professionals. Many trainers and human resource professionals do not have formal education and experience in this field, and did not select HRD as their original occupation, but transferred into the field as subject matter experts with preservice educational backgrounds in occupations outside HRD (Kaeter, 1995; Lapides, 1991; McCullough, 1987). Although there has been significant growth over the last decade in the number of universities that are awarding postgraduate degrees in subjects related to HRD (Kaeter, 1995), a 1993 *Training* study suggests that 55 percent of those trainers surveyed were working as trainers without a college degree (16 percent) or with a bachelor's degree (39 percent). Thirty-eight percent of those surveyed held master's degrees, and fewer than 7 percent had a Ph.D. degree. For those practitioners who may be ineligible to pursue courses without a commitment to seek bachelor's or master's degrees, nondegree certificate and certification programs may offer a cost-effective and timely educational alternative.

In sum, given all of these trends, it becomes evident that human resource professionals, like other professional employees, are not immune from changes affecting their livelihood. The growth of nondegree certificate and certification programs in training and human resource development, and professional certification in the human resource management field may be indicative of the perceived need to remain competitive and competent. These programs may also present an alternative option for timely and continual professional development.

The Arguments for Certification

The arguments supporting certification are as well documented as the arguments against certification (Booth, 1984; Coscarelli, 1984; Galbraith and Gilley, 1985; Gilley, 1986; Gilley and Galbraith, 1986; James, 1992; White, 1992; Wiley, 1995). Opponents of certification contend that certification has several negative implications for the field of adult education and human resource development. They are the diversity and extensiveness of the field (James, 1992); the lack of a common body of knowledge and the difficulty of establishing competence criteria and measurement standards; the potential restriction of the labor supply; and the financial and human costs, legal implications, and regulatory processes associated with the administration of certification (Galbraith and Gilley, 1985). These issues are not trivial, nor should they be dismissed; however, they should not overshadow the positive implications associated with certification. These negative implications are refuted and the positive implications of certification are discussed in the following section.

Refuting the Arguments Against Certification. The field of adult education and human resource development is fragmented, diverse, and interdisciplinary. A common body of knowledge may not exist for the entire field, and therefore, a single, comprehensive certification program representing the interests of all adult educators and human resource developers may not be possible. However, certification may be plausible in certain specific areas of the field, such as training and human resource development.

Lack of a Common Body of Knowledge. ASTD provided a set of competency standards for the field in 1983 and in 1989 and continues to examine the evolving roles of human resource development practitioners. These efforts, although important first steps, are frustrated by lack of a common body of knowledge and by the broad scope of practices associated with the field (Watkins, 1995). Watkins (1990, p. 181) argues that "we need to standardize not our curriculum, but our vision for the field." Given the rapid changes occurring in the workplace, defining competencies for what practitioners are currently doing in the field as opposed to what they might be or ought to be doing may rigidify HRD practice rather than advance it. According to Watkins (1990, p. 181), "It is more important to agree on a common set of values that might characterize ethical practice, on a common understanding of what represents an optimal career ladder for the field, and on the role of HRD graduate programs in professionalizing the field than to standardize it." Certificate and certification programs have the potential to influence the development and professionalization of the field by promoting an integrated vision for the field that embraces a common set of values that characterizes ethical practice. Once a vision is established, a common body of knowledge may emerge. Existing certificate and certification programs may offer a perspective on what professionals in the field perceive to be critical to effective practice, given the changes occurring in the workplace.

Restricting the Labor Supply. One of the functions that certification can serve in real-world labor markets is that of restricting the labor supply, or gatekeeping for the field, which is an activity that is perceived to limit the entry of qualified professionals (Galbraith and Gilley, 1986). Gatekeeping may appear to be elitist as it has the potential to cartelize a field by preventing marginal workers from identifying with a particular occupation. However, Hochberger (1993, p. 32) asks "Isn't there *something* we can do to expose the charlatans in our business? Isn't there some way to drive these people out of the corporate-training field and to restore some professionalism?" Embracing certification may be one of the answers. It may not expose every charlatan in our field, but it may serve as a differentiating factor in selection decisions.

Administrative and Regulatory Issues. There are numerous administrative and regulatory issues that must be addressed by a credentialing agency offering certification. However, to avoid pursuing the establishment of a certification agency on the basis of these issues would be unfortunate, as there are agency models in other professions that could serve as a benchmark. In the field of training and human resource development, three associations offer workable models that could be used as a guide. They are the Ontario Society for Training and Development in Canada, the Society for Human Resource Management, and the International Board of Standards for Training, Performance, and Instruction (Smith, 1994).

Why Certify? Positive Implications of Certification. The benefits of certification are examined from three perspectives: the individual seeking certification, the organization, and the field, discipline, or profession promoting certification (Wiley, 1995).

The Individual. For the individual seeking certification, the benefits include the mastery of a body of knowledge; personal and professional recognition of the attainment of a certification designation; the potential for career advancement and pay incentives; a timely and cost-effective approach to professional development; an opportunity to develop a network of professionals with whom ideas, experiences, and best practices can be shared, and an avenue to pursue lifelong learning for personal and professional development. In a workplace that will be increasingly reliant on an individual's development through self-directed learning endeavors, certificate and certification programs may become a critical external resource to many practitioners.

The Organization. For the organization employing certified practitioners, certification provides a demonstrated commitment by the employee to personal and professional development. Certification may also assist in the selection process to increase the likelihood of staffing HR functions with qualified professionals. Although more empirical research is needed to assess performance among certified and noncertified professionals, preliminary results of a research study found that payback times on certification expenses were typically less than nine months and productivity was higher among certified personnel in the information technology field (Merrill, 1995).

The Field, Discipline, or Profession. According to the Department of Labor, certification and the existence of a credentialing agency is one criterion that distinguishes a profession from an occupation. Certification is often viewed as one of the ways in which a field or discipline can be advanced, and one of the ways in which a field can develop and maintain professional and competent practitioners. The development of a common body of knowledge, or an integrated vision for the field that serves as a framework for certification, may also provide direction in the design of college and university curricula. Certification can provide guidance to junior practitioners and can encourage senior practitioners to update their knowledge in order to remain competitive.

Conclusions

As this chapter has illustrated, certification is alive and well in the human resource management field and its various specializations, and it is alive and well in training and human resource development despite the absence of a formal certification process. The formation and longevity of nondegree training and human resource development certificate and certification programs is indicative of the growing demand for such programs among HRD practitioners. This increasing demand, perhaps fueled by the changes in the workplace and in the HRD field, suggests it might be time for these associations and university-sponsored certificate and certification program administrators to join forces in a collaborative manner to address the issues associated with certification of training and human resource development practitioners for the advancement of the field. Accordingly, certification continues to be a rich area for future research initiatives and continued exploration.

References

Booth, B. "Certification—Beyond Reason." *Performance and Instruction*, 1984, 23 (1), 19.

Bratton, B., and Hildebrand, M. "Plain Talk About Professional Certification." *Instructional Innovator*, 1980, 25 (9), 22–24.

Bridges, W. *JobShift*. Reading, Mass.: Addison-Wesley, 1994.

Carnevale, A. P., and Carnevale, E. S. "Growth Patterns in Workplace Training." *Training and Development*, May 1994, pp. S22–S28.

Cervero, R. M. "Adult and Continuing Education Should Strive for Professionalization." In M. W. Galbraith and B. R. Sisco (eds.), *Confronting Controversies in Challenging Times: A Call for Action*. New Directions for Adult and Continuing Education, no. 54. San Francisco: Jossey-Bass, 1992.

Cherrington, D. J., and Leonard, B. "HR Pioneers' Long Road to Certification." *HRMagazine*, 1993, 38 (11), 63–75.

Collins, M. "Adult and Continuing Education Should Resist Further Professionalization." In M. W. Galbraith and B. R. Sisco (eds.), *Confronting Controversies in Challenging Times: A Call for Action*. New Directions for Adult and Continuing Education, no. 54. San Francisco: Jossey-Bass, 1992.

Coscarelli, W. "Arguments for Certification." *Performance and Instruction*, 1984, 23 (1), 21.

Filipczak, B. "Certifiable!" *Training*, 1995a, 32 (8), 38–42.

Filipczak, B. "The Fever Spreads." *Training*, 1995b, 32 (8), 40.

Galbraith, M. W., and Gilley, J. W. "An Examination of Professional Certification." *Lifelong Learning: An Omnibus of Practice and Research*, 1985, 9 (2), 12–15.

Galbraith, M. W., and Gilley, J. W. *Professional Certification: Implications for Adult Education and HRD*. Columbus, Ohio: ERIC Clearinghouse on Adult, Career, and Vocational Education, 1986.

Gaudet, C. H., and Kotrlik, J. W. "Status of HRD Certificate Program Development." *Human Resource Development Quarterly*, 1995, 6 (1), 91–99.

Gilley, J. W. "Defining a Profession: Does HRD Measure Up?" *Personnel Administrator,* 1986, *31* (1), 14–18.

Gilley, J. W., and Galbraith, M. W. "Examining Professional Certification." *Training and Development,* 1986, *40* (6), 60–61.

Handy, C. *The Age of Unreason.* Boston: Harvard Business School Press, 1990.

Hochberger, J. "Ship of Charlatans." *Training,* Nov. 1993, pp. 32–35.

Holt, M. E. "A Rationale for Certificate Programs." In M. E. Holt and G. J. Lopos (eds.), *Perspectives on Educational Certificate Programs.* New Directions for Adult and Continuing Education, no. 52. San Francisco: Jossey-Bass, 1991.

James, W. B. "Professional Certification Is Not Needed in Adult and Continuing Education." In M. W. Galbraith and B. R. Sisco (eds.), *Confronting Controversies in Challenging Times: A Call for Action.* New Directions for Adult and Continuing Education, no. 54. San Francisco: Jossey-Bass, 1992.

Kaeter, M. "HRD Degrees: Who Needs Them?" *Training,* Nov. 1995, pp. 65–74.

Lapides, J. "Continuing Professional Development." In N. M. Dixon and J. Hinkelman (eds.), *The Academic Guide.* Alexandria, Va.: American Society for Training and Development, 1991.

Lapp, H. J. "Important and Meaningful Distinctions Between Qualification and Certification." *Performance and Instruction,* 1992, *31* (9), 3–8.

Lee, C. "Certification for Trainers: Thumbs Up." *Training,* 1986, *23* (1), 56–64.

Lopos, G. J. "Certificate Programs: Alternative Ways to Career Advancement and Social Mobility?" In M. E. Holt and G. J. Lopos (eds.), *Perspectives on Educational Certificate Programs.* New Directions for Adult and Continuing Education, no. 52. San Francisco: Jossey-Bass, 1991.

McCullough, R. C. "Professional Development." In R. L. Craig (ed.), *Training and Development Handbook.* (3rd ed.) New York: McGraw-Hill, 1987.

McLagan, P. "Great Ideas Revisited." *Training and Development,* 1996, *50* (1), 60–65.

Merrill, K. "New Training Study Bolsters Arguments for Vendor-Authorized Certification Programs." *Computer Reseller News,* 1995, (656), 62.

Morrow, L. "The Temping of America." *Time,* Feb. 8, 1993, pp. 40–41.

"1995 Industry Report." *Training,* 1995, *32* (10), 37–82.

Nonaka, I. "The Knowledge-Creating Company." *Harvard Business Review,* Nov/Dec 1991, pp. 96–104.

Parmerlee, D. "Certification Through Professional Development." *Marketing Research,* 1991, *3* (4), 63–65.

Settle, T. J. "Certification Programs for Business and Industry." In M. E. Holt and G. J. Lopos (eds.), *Perspectives on Educational Certificate Programs.* New Directions for Adult and Continuing Education, no. 52. San Francisco: Jossey-Bass, 1991.

Smith, T. R. "Exploring the Structure of Human Resource/Training and Development Non-Degree Certificate Programs at U.S. Colleges and Universities and the Perceived Needs of Practitioners." Unpublished doctoral dissertation, Texas A & M University, 1994.

Stata, R. "Organizational Learning—The Key to Management Innovation." *Sloan Management Review,* 1989, *30* (3), 63–74.

"Trends That Will Influence Workplace Learning and Performance in the Next Five Years." *Training and Development,* 1994, *48* (5), S29–S32.

Ulrich, D., Brockbank, W., Yeung, A. K., and Lake, D. G. "Human Resource Competencies: An Empirical Assessment." *Human Resource Management,* 1995, *34* (4), 473–495.

Watkins, K. E. "A Common Body of Knowledge Is Nonsense in a Field in Search of Itself." *Human Resource Development Quarterly,* 1990, *1* (2), 181–185.

Watkins, K. E. "Workplace Learning: Changing Times, Changing Practices." In W. F. Spikes (ed.), *Workplace Learning.* New Directions for Adult and Continuing Education, no. 68. San Francisco: Jossey-Bass, 1995.

Watkins, K. E., and Marsick, V. J. *Sculpting the Learning Organization: Lessons in the Art and Science of Systematic Change.* San Francisco: Jossey-Bass, 1993.

White, B. A. "Professional Certification Is a Needed Option for Adult and Continuing Education." In M. W. Galbraith and B. R. Sisco (eds.), *Confronting Controversies in Challenging Times: A Call for Action.* New Directions for Adult and Continuing Education, no. 54. San Francisco: Jossey-Bass, 1992.

Wiley, C. "The Certified HR Professional." *HRMagazine,* 1992a, *37* (8), 77–84.

Wiley, C. "The Wave of the Future: Certification in Human Resource Management." *Human Resource Management Review,* 1992b, *2* (2), 157–170.

Wiley, C. "Reexamining Professional Certification in Human Resource Management." *Human Resource Management,* 1995, *34* (2), 269–289.

Wilkinson, E. S., Jr. "An Overview of Certification Programs in the Purchasing and Materials Management Field." *International Journal of Purchasing,* 1992, *28* (1), 34–39.

ANDREA D. ELLINGER is a doctoral candidate in adult education at the University of Georgia and is program administrator for the Department of Adult Education's Certification in Training and Human Resource Development Program.

PART FIVE

Do Organizations Learn?

Moving from the psychological literature that identifies a group psychology or mental state to the organizational literature that defines the collective nature of organizations, this chapter develops a model of learning at the organizational level.

Of Course Organizations Learn!

Karen E. Watkins

Anyone who has ever been part of a group or team that has suddenly become capable of thinking and acting together has experienced a synergistic state that evidences that groups can and do learn. Yet, Freud has argued that individual and group psychology cannot be absolutely differentiated because individual psychology is a function of the individual's relationship to another person or object (in Bion, 1961). Similarly, Jung discusses the idea of a group intelligence about which he has said that the larger the group, the more stupid it becomes as it makes differences disadvantages and stresses average qualities in its members (Fordham, 1953). Janis' (1972) notion of groupthink and earlier notions of mob psychology carry this same connotation; groups are capable of a collective intelligence, but this intelligence is not necessarily greater than individual intelligence. This chapter argues that organizations can learn, but this learning cannot be disassociated from individual learning; and organizational learning must address the group's tendencies toward helplessness and conformity by encouraging collaboration, empowerment, and critical reflection.

Does the Organization Learn?

Even as a host of scholars have attempted to understand how organizations learn (Meyer, 1982; Watkins and Marsick, 1992, 1993; Argyris and Schön, 1978, 1996; March and Olsen, 1976; Fiol and Lyles, 1985), individuals question whether an organization learns. After all, if learning is a relatively permanent change in the brain's chemical makeup, what would the analogue be at the organizational level? Would the organization be able to do something different, have a new memory, or alter its attitudes or beliefs? Can an organization literally *do* anything? Do we anthropomorphize organizations when we say they learn?

Argyris and Schön (1978, 1996) note that organizational learning is not the same thing as individual learning, nor is it the same as when top management learns for the organization. Although it is not really individual learning, organizations learn only through the experience and actions of individuals. Fiol and Lyles (1985) argue that "though individual learning is important to organizations, organizational learning is not simply the sum of each member's learning. Organizations, unlike individuals, develop and maintain learning systems that not only influence their immediate members but are then transmitted to others by way of organization history and norms" (p. 804). Nonaka (1994) states that "an organization cannot create knowledge without individuals. The organization supports creative individuals or provides a context for such individuals to create knowledge. Organizational knowledge creation, therefore, should be understood in terms of a process that 'organizationally' amplifies the knowledge created by individuals, and crystallizes it as a part of the knowledge network of the organization" (p. 17). Organizations learn when individuals inquire into a problematic situation on the organization's behalf. "In order to become organizational, the learning that results from organizational inquiry must become embedded in the images of organization held in its members' minds and/or in the epistemological artifacts (the maps, memories, and programs) embedded in the organizational environment" (Argyris and Schön, 1996, p. 16).

Organizations learn when they actually retain, crystallize, or embed new practices, values, or understandings; that is, when they really change. Most of the changes in organizations do not really change anything. New labels appear on old practices; lip service is given to new ideas but no new skills are acquired by the organizations' members. Individuals may experience sea changes in some of these nonchanges. Other changes may make less difference to individuals in the organization, yet make a major difference at the organizational level. It is this changed capacity at the organizational level that constitutes organizational learning.

For example, when an organization closes down an entire plant or division, has it learned? It depends, but most likely, it has not. Most likely, this is the same strategy the organization has always used to deal with market downturns. When General Motors created the Saturn plant, on the other hand, something had changed. When an organization learns new approaches to managing market instability, such as employee ownership, co-ops, or entrepreneurial divisions (for example, Texas Instruments' custom manufacturing group), it is learning. When an organization tries something and it does not work, it has learned one of the many ways not to solve a problem. When an organization alters the fundamental relationships between people in the organization, as with self-managed work teams, it is learning. Yet, if the organization attempts such approaches as flattening the hierarchy or cross-functional teams, but within the experiment the *pattern* of relationships remains stratified with simply new leaders, little has been learned. People have merely played musical chairs in the old paradigm. Employee empowerment strategies that do not end up in real differences in employees' collective sense of autonomy and actual power to make decisions about the conditions under which they work will not lead to real learning.

Embedded is therefore a key word in understanding learning at the organizational level. It involves a systematic effort to capture in some permanent way the learning of individuals and groups. A learning organization must stand ready to do what the Japanese call *saving the gains,* without overloading the system too much, to reap the benefits of learning. The notion of embeddedness is best captured in the concept of organizational memory. *Organizational memory* refers to stored information from an organization's history, such as knowledge about what has worked in the past when certain types of problems occur. The importance of technology for creating on-line processes for capturing this learning must be underscored. For example, electronic bulletin board programs allow engineers in Australia to pose a problem on the system in the middle of the night that can be answered by morning from anywhere in the world. More important, with a workforce that is increasingly contingent, outsourced, or downsized, an organization risks losing its intellectual capital if it allows learning to remain in individuals rather than capturing it in organizational routines and databases.

The Learning Cycle

A learning organization is one in which learning and work are integrated in an ongoing and systematic fashion to support continuous improvement at the individual, group, and organizational levels. The learning cycle integrates human thinking and human doing into the collective enterprise.

Learning at the Individual Level. One way to clarify the nature of learning at the organizational level is to contrast it with how individuals learn from experience. Elsewhere (Marsick and Watkins, 1990; Watkins and Marsick, 1992, 1993), we developed a theory of informal and incidental learning in the workplace in which we noted that most learning takes place either on the job, in informal settings, or coincident to other work tasks. This, we think, leads to a need for new approaches to learning in the workplace.

Learning at the Organizational Level. The word *organization* comes from the Greek *organon,* meaning tool or instrument, hence the notion that organizations are devices invented by people to aid in performing some kind of collective goal-oriented activity (Morgan, 1986). People create organizations as a tool to enable goal accomplishment. That tool makes concerted action possible. What is most significant at the organizational level is that learning is now a collective, interdependent experience.

A jolt or a surprise triggered the organizational learning cycle in Meyer's research (1982). Other scholars have suggested that a learning cycle is triggered in the organization by new experiences (March and Olsen, 1976), by the detection of error or a mismatch between what was intended and what was produced (Argyris and Schön, 1978), by the gap between current reality and one's vision (Senge, 1990), and by designing future scenarios. It is the gap between current reality and vision that is the source of the creative tension that produces learning. Inconsistency disorients, unfreezes, or destabilizes a situation and stimulates learning. The stages of the learning cycle are the same at the organizational level as for individuals, but learning is now the result of an interactive, interdependent process.

Learning is triggered by organizational jolts or surprises such as a new regulation, a new competitor, market downturns, new technology, customer dissatisfaction or new demands, a new idea, a new vision, or some other change in the status quo. The culture of the organization serves as a filter, selecting what the organization pays attention to. Through its system of functions, the organization arrives at a strategy for responding to the change. What determines the effectiveness of this strategy is the ability of the organization to act cohesively. This requires both alignment of vision about what to do, shared meaning about intentions, and the capacity to work together cross-functionally. This collaborative capacity leads to collective action. Once the organization responds, individuals and departments make assumptions about the effectiveness of that response. In a quality managed environment, these assumptions are increasingly databased. At any rate, there are consequences for both individuals and organizations from the actions taken. If the response has been to integrate a new technology, for example, considerable skill learning is required at the individual level, and the organization has a new capacity. Learning, finally, is the net result of this cycle. What is learned is what the organization retains as a new capacity, a new understanding of what doesn't work, a new procedure or technology, and so forth. In a learning organization, the organization systematically works to capture and embed new learning in a manner that facilitates widespread dissemination of that learning both for others already in the organization who would benefit from this knowledge and for future employees.

Learning at the organizational level is not the sum of many people learning. Yet, individuals carry within them a microcosmic portrait of the organization. Through them, we detect changes in the organization's mental models, shared values, and memory. Learning by individuals is necessary for the organization to change, but not sufficient. When individuals increase their capacity to learn, either through workplace literacy programs, retraining, cross-training, educational programs, and so on, they (collectively) enhance the overall capacity of the organization to learn. In short, individual learning is related to organizational learning though not equal to it, and potentially (though not necessarily) interdependent with it.

What Changes? What Is Different When the Organization Learns?
What, then, is the metric by which we test whether or not an organization has learned? In fact, organizations learn all of the time. Aren't they therefore learning organizations? A learning organization is one that has embedded the capacity to adapt or to respond quickly and in novel ways while working to remove barriers to learning. They increase their capacity to learn by making changes

in the four systems that influence learning: strategy, structure, slack, and ideology. Rules, memory, values, the system of relationships or structure, the underlying dynamic or pattern that characterizes the organization, all may change.

Fritz Heider (1958) said that learning occurs when three conditions are met: the learners CAN learn whatever it is we ask them to learn; the learners WANT to learn it, and the learners, because they believe that they can succeed, will TRY to learn. At the organizational level, this would lead us to assess the capacity of the organization to learn. Therefore, organizations that are engaged in workplace literacy initiatives in order to change the threshold of skill in the organization, for example, are taking one step toward creating the possibility of a learning organization. Systemwide skills assessments and training strategically targeted to skill gaps are strategies that hold promise.

Motivation, the *want* in learning, has also been studied at the organizational level. Organizations that have a wide range of options for both recognizing and rewarding achievement, for linking pay with individual and team needs and performance, and for funding learning, have created methods for motivating continuous learning. Work redesign and experiments with self-directed or self-managed teams also may create the motivation to learn by making work challenging.

Approaches that appear to encourage the organization and its members to try are those that focus on empowerment and employee involvement. Structures that encourage dependency lead to learned helplessness. Under these conditions, people do not try new things. As one person put it, "In this organization, there are nine people waiting to lop off the branch when you go out on a limb. Is it any wonder no one wants to sign up for this change effort?"

At the organizational level, more collaborative structures (not necessarily but often more decentralized or flatter structures) enhance the organization's ability to learn. Boundary spanning, in the form of encouraging employees to meet with customers or benchmark their work against other organizations and other collaborative or cross-functional (cross-organizational boundaries) endeavors, enhances learning. *Slack* is another key to whether an organization either has the capacity to learn (hence the focus on literacy and skill acquisition to increase the available repertoire of skill available in the organization to respond to unforeseen problems) or will try to learn. An organization that has no financial, technological, or human reserves (that is, no slack) has no spare resources to learn or to try new things. Carnevale, Gainer, and Villet (1990) called the internal training organization "the little R & D." The learning organization systematically nourishes its big and little research and development systems to ensure that the organization will continue to be able to create new possibilities and to support them with new skills.

Some educational philosophers believe that education is a process of making space (Lewin, 1951). Whether one is challenging existing prejudices, thereby making room for new beliefs; increasing individuals' ability to think critically, thereby making space for challenging old ideas while testing the merits of new ideas; or teaching new skills; the net effect is that individuals have more room to act and to think. Freedom of movement at the organizational level might be accomplished by learning to work collaboratively, because it extends an organization's capacity to achieve unified action on common goals or problems. Learning to think systemically may also ensure greater space for free movement because this allows more individuals in the organization to have an accurate picture of the interdependence of the parts of the organization, the people, and the actions taken. Software programs such as that developed by Jay Forrester at M.I.T. called "I Think," which technologically enhance the organization's ability to systemically model components of the organization and to see the effects of alternative responses on the whole system, hold promise here. Finally, the approaches with the greatest potential to enhance the space of free movement in an organization are those that empower all members of the organization. Autonomy means having the power to act on one's own initiative. Rigid structures constrain autonomy and collaboration, as do the tacit control-oriented and authoritarian belief systems of the organization. A more democratic culture would help reach this balance between collaboration and autonomy.

Learning occurs developmentally from making mistakes; beginning with awkward hit-and-miss, trial-and-error achievement; to minimal performance; and finally all the way to high performance. A climate of public humiliation, an atmosphere of criticism, or the use of punitive performance appraisals are deadly for learning. Learning is squelched in the little incidental moments when, for example, a quality team mentions tentatively what it wants to work on and a top manager says that it will never work. Hence, culture filters, shapes, and constrains learning.

Learning is opportunistic. Those who develop the sense of when they are in a teachable moment and when others have shut down make effective teachers. At the organizational level, this takes the form of experiments in teaching managers to be facilitators, coaches, educators, and guides.

A Final Dilemma

One individual raised a significant concern about organizational learning. He noted that in his organization, people love it when we say that we are engaged in an organizational change, because they can then distance themselves from responsibility for taking any action by saying, It's not my responsibility, it's the organization's.

Perhaps a better way to look at this issue is to explore what individuals must do to create a learning organization and what the organization must provide to support individuals. Table 10.1 illustrates this balance between individual action and the concomitant organizational support systems needed.

Organizations can and do learn. What they learn, however, may not advance either the organizations or the society in which they operate. Individuals will continue to bear the responsibility for monitoring what is learned

Table 10.1. Relationship Between Individual Action and Organizational Support

Strategy	Individual	Organization
Learn continually	Invest in learning on one's own, toward future skills demands	Provide learning resources, funds, training on self-directed learning; measure future skill requirements; capture learning gains
Change rapidly	Develop personal resilience and knowledge of the change process	Ensure that every member of the organization learns change management techniques; scan the environment and create early-warning systems regarding impending changes; communicate changes made and anticipated
Improve information flow	Learn skills of dialogue and inquiry, information search and retrieval skills	Create culture of safety, technological and nontechnological systems for sharing information
Take initiative	Develop a systems view of one's work, cross train; push one's comfort zone and redefine one's authority to act	Empower individuals to make decisions in their work arena; remove barriers to taking action; support cross-training and systems thinking
Invent the future	Seek customer data; conduct research and experiments to improve processes, products, and services; read; benchmark competitors	Reward suggestions and ideas for improvements

and for designing systems and policies to support and encourage continuous learning and improvement. Organizations require supportive learning cultures that give individuals the authority to act and balance individual, organizational, and societal needs.

References

Argyris, C., and Schön, D. *Organizational Learning: A Theory of Action Perspective.* San Francisco: Jossey-Bass, 1978.

Argyris, C., and Schön, D. *Organizational Learning II: Theory, Method, and Practice.* Reading, Mass.: Addison-Wesley, 1996.

Bion, W. *Experiences in Groups.* New York: Basic Books, 1961.

Carnevale, A. P., Gainer, L., and Villet, J. *Training in America: The Organization and Strategic Role of Training.* San Francisco: Jossey-Bass, 1990.

Fiol, M. C., and Lyles, M. A. "Organizational Learning." *Academy of Management Review,* 1985, *10* (4), 803–813.

Fordham, F. *An Introduction to Jung's Psychology.* Harmondsworth, Middlesex, England: Penguin, 1953.

Heider, F. *The Psychology of Interpersonal Relations.* New York: Wiley, 1958.

Janis, I. L. *Victims of Groupthink*. Boston: Houghton Mifflin, 1972.

Lewin, K. *Field Theory in Social Science: Selected Theoretical Papers*. (D. Cartwright, ed.). New York: Harper & Row, 1951.

March, J. G., and Olsen, J. P. *Ambiguity and Choice in Organizations*. Norway: Universitets-forlaget, 1976.

Marsick, V. J., and Watkins, K. E. *Informal and Incidental Learning in the Workplace*. London: Routledge, 1990.

Meyer, A. "Adapting to environmental jolts." *Administrative Science Quarterly*, 1982, 27 (4), 515–537.

Morgan, G. *Images of Organizations*. Newbury Park: Sage, 1986.

Nonaka, I. "A dynamic theory of organizational knowledge creation." *Organization Science* 1994, V (1), 14–37.

Senge, P. *The Fifth Discipline: The Art and Practice of the Learning Organization*. New York: Doubleday Currency, 1990.

Watkins, K. E., and Marsick, V. J. "Towards a Theory of Informal and Incidental Learning in Organizations." *International Journal of Lifelong Education*, 1992, 11 (4), 287–300.

Watkins, K. E., and Marsick, V. J. *Sculpting the Learning Organization: Lessons in the Art and Science of Systematic Change*. San Francisco: Jossey-Bass, 1993.

KAREN E. WATKINS is professor of adult education and director of HRD programs at the University of Georgia in Athens.

The lukasa, an African mnemonic device, illustrates the way in which individual meaning making enables adults to interpret and shape organizational meaning making.

Individuals Who Learn Create Organizations That Learn

Victoria J. Marsick, Peter G. Neaman

Individual learning is central to organizational learning. The *lukasa,* an African mnemonic device, is used to illustrate the way in which individuals interpret and shape organizational memory. First, the paradox of organizational learning is examined to understand the role of individual learning within it. Adult learning theory is then used to shed light on how such learning occurs. Finally, conditions are identified that distort the way in which individual learning could contribute effectively to organizational learning.

Organizational Memory

Some fifty miles west of the western shore of Lake Tanganyika in southeastern Zaire live the Luba, one of the major art-producing peoples of sub-Saharan Africa—and originators of the lukasa. The lukasa is perhaps the most impressive example known of an object that is encoded in "organizational memory." Recollection of their collective past is a dominant force in Luba culture, powerfully informing consideration of, and legitimizing, not only current events but also prospective action (Nooter, 1993).

Like many Luba artifacts, the lukasa is a mnemonic device. "[A] handheld, flat wooden object studded with beads and pins, or covered with incised or carved ideograms" (Roberts, 1996, p. 285), it holds layers of meaning: medicinal, architectural, geographical, genealogical, and biographical. "During . . . rituals to induct rulers into office, a lukasa is used to teach sacred lore about culture heroes, clan migrations, and the introduction of sacred rule; to suggest the spatial positioning of activities and offices within the kingdom or inside a royal compound; and to order the sacred prerogatives of the officials concerning contact with earth spirits and exploitation of natural resources" (Roberts, 1996, p. 286).

Roberts (1996) explains that lukasas are always "read" by "rigorously trained 'men of memory'" of the Mbudye society (p. 286). Because of the fluidity of thought permitted by its "multi-referenced iconography"—for example, "lines of beads [may] refer to journeys, roads and migrations"—the lukasa is actually a more potent mnemonic device than writing, serving "not [to] symbolize thought so much as [to] stimulate it" (p. 286). Thus, interpretation of the lukasa is richly contextual, varying from reader to reader and with contingencies of the occasion, demonstrating that there is "not an absolute or collective memory" of the Luba past, "but many memories, and many histories" (p. 286).

The Luba learned as a collective when individuals interpreted the lukasa in order to make sense of new experiences; additions were made to the lukasa to represent new data of significance to the community. The lukasa carried with it rich meaning from the past, but the individuals who interpreted events on a specific occasion brought to bear their gifts as meaning makers in the present. Thus, the collective system did selectively learn and pass on its learning, and it could only do so through the active agency of individuals—those who were designated as official interpreters, as well as others who listened and acted on what they heard.

Organizational Learning as Paradox

By asking a fundamental question—"What is an organization that it may learn?"—Argyris and Schön (1996, p. 3) highlight a paradox of organizational learning. Organizations are not living beings, so how can they learn? Schön (1983) captures the paradox: "it is unclear what we mean when we treat the term 'organization' as the subject of a sentence that has 'learning' as its predicate" (p. 115). Argyris and Schön (1996) think through the way in which a system might be capable of learning. They point out that "by establishing rule-governed ways of deciding, delegating, and setting the boundaries of membership, a collectivity becomes an organization capable of acting" (p. 9). Organizations "belong to the genus of systems in which individuals cooperate to perform tasks that arise repetitively" (p. 10). They maintain that organizations are not ephemeral, but act on a continuing basis over time, and thus, build up systems, policies, procedures, and cultures.

Argyris and Schön conclude that, in a collectivity, when "members can *act* for it, then it may be said to learn when its members *learn* for it, carrying out a process of inquiry that results in a learning product" (p. 11). Yet, even as they conclude that individuals can learn on behalf of the organization, they underscore the difficulty many have in accepting this notion: "To the distinguished social scientists who were repelled by the idea when we first broached it in the early 1970s, 'organizational learning' seemed to smell of some quasi-mystical, Hegelian personification of the collectivity. Surely, they felt, it is *indi-*

viduals who may be said to learn, just as to think, reason, or hold opinions. To them, it seemed paradoxical, if not perverse, to attribute learning to *organizations*" (p. 4).

In speaking of organizational systems for cooperation and control—in this case, those of a hypothetical cooperative—Schön (1983) observes that "each individual must generate an image of the cooperative system on which his or her own performance depends. He or she may make use of organizational artifacts such as maps, programs, and memories" (p. 117). Using these artifacts, "individuals refresh the private images that enable them to adjust their behavior to the behavior of others in the system" (p. 118). However, Schön also underscores the gaps that occur when individuals interpret organizational imagery in specific situations: "General principles do not decide particular cases. The new worker will still have to complete by his own behavior the incomplete description of task performance that is all the organization can give him" (p. 118). This last speaks to the critical contribution of individual meaning making in the organizational setting.

A more productive focus, then, is not whether or not organizational learning is possible, but rather, how it may be possible, and what role individuals play in its creation. Adult learning theory sheds light on the question of how individuals make this happen.

Adult Learning Theory Perspective

Brookfield (1986, p. 60) emphasizes that "ultimately, it is individuals who learn, not groups. . . . Even when one is a member of a learning group, one does not transfer part of one's consciousness to the group. There is no group mind, no separate entity that is learning over and above the individual learning undertaken by each group member." Brookfield emphasizes one side of the argument; that is, that only individuals learn. His stance is characteristic of the liberal, humanistic stream of adult education. Based on the thinking of humanistic psychologists such as Rogers (1967), the focus is first and foremost on individual self-development. It has culminated in self-directed learning theories that speak to ways in which individuals define and manage their own learning through learning projects. The humanistic tradition has been criticized because of its single-minded focus on individual fulfillment in absence of attention to the social-cultural-political context of learners. Social inequities privilege some and disadvantage others in the setting of learning goals and the distribution of resources to pursue these ends (Candy, 1991; Welton, 1995).

Individuals learn in a social context. In addition, they can act as agents for collective learning that leads to change. However, to do so, adults must consciously interpret and critique social norms that they encounter as they make meaning (Jarvis, 1987). Forces in an organization often conspire to mold individuals, rather than to liberate them to freely reinterpret meaning when this reinterpretation might challenge prevailing power and social norms (Freire, 1974; Mezirow, 1991; Welton, 1995). In organizations, individuals try to make sense of the experiences they have in pursuit of their work. As they do so, they either uncritically use socialized, collective meanings from the organization to shape their thinking, or else—ideally—they can challenge these socialized views and proactively shape new norms through their interactions with others.

Learning theory that has most been drawn on to understand meaning making in the workplace can ultimately be traced back to John Dewey (1938). Although Dewey was interested in progressive social action, workplace learning theory emphasizes Dewey's contribution to individual problem solving. Dewey's interest in the scientific method as a basis for learning from experience was more integrated than many simple problem-solving models imply. He feared that some might interpret his focus on the scientific method too narrowly as "the special technique of laboratory research" (p. 87). Dewey conceived the scientific method more broadly as "the only authentic means at our command for getting at the significance of our everyday experiences of the world in which we live" (p. 88).

Watkins and Marsick (1993) illustrate the way in which individuals learn from experience as they encounter and solve problems. This model is based on Dewey, the social psychology of Kurt Lewin, and Argyris and Schön (1996). Learning begins with internal or external triggers that stimulate a response. Triggers include surprises, discrepancies between anticipated and actual experience, accidents, or challenges. Learners then review alternative responses, select a strategy, and act based on their cognitive and affective understanding of the meaning of the initial trigger. The strategy then either works or does not work as expected. Between the initial trigger and the determination of a strategy is an implicit filtering of the information through one's selective perception, values, beliefs, and framing of the situation. These filters, as Mezirow (1991) explains, are strongly influenced by social and cultural norms that are often unconsciously and uncritically accepted. Actions are constrained by capacity to act—both in terms of actual skills and perceptions of capability or authority to act. Action can be followed by a review of results, though this does not always take place, as well as a deeper digging for the real reasons behind both intended and unintended consequences. Finally, out of these consequences and attributions about them, learners selectively make meaning of the experience and retain these cognitive constructs as what is learned from the experience.

The model is neither straightforward nor prescriptive: steps such as observation and reflection are interwoven throughout various phases of the model, and the learning process varies because of the situation in which people find themselves. The problem-solving cycle is embedded within a subsurface cycle composed of the beliefs, values, and assumptions that guide action at each stage. The subsurface cycle is not readily accessible. So, as learners move around the problem-solving cycle, they need to work hard to identify and acknowledge tacit beliefs, values, assumptions, contextual factors, and unintended outcomes that might shape their understanding of the situation.

Many models of individual learning do not sufficiently emphasize the way in which individuals often fall victim to taken-for-granted messages transmitted by powerful forces in their lives and society when they make meaning of their experience. Moreover, challenges in organizations are, by and large, social challenges embedded in socially constructed realities. But often, organizations are sensitive about critiques of many of these norms, even if they say they are not. The individualistic nature of our society also encourages people to focus on their own learning, in isolation of that of others, and learning models do not press sufficiently to change this orientation.

Individual learning and meaning making is inextricably intertwined with any process of organizational learning. But learning theory often focuses on the individual and does not pay sufficient attention to how the individual can more effectively surface, critique, and use new insights about his or her socialization to proactively influence organizational learning. Mezirow (1991) does attempt to do this for individuals, as do Argyris and Schön (1996) in their theory of action science.

Individuals are central to new learning because only individuals can think anew . . . even though an individual's capacity to engage in fresh thinking or to influence the organization's thinking may be limited by many factors. Such constraints may well result in the tyranny of the collective over individuals and their ability to create systems that live up to the potential of either individual or organizational learning.

Conditions Limiting the Individual's Role in Organizational Learning

Systems-level learning is not, by its inherent nature, a threat to individuals. Organizations are dependent on the learning of individuals, and to a greater or lesser degree, must encourage and support such learning if the system is to learn. However, there are a number of flaws in the way in which organizational learning systems are implemented that can act as a threat to the learning of individuals and to their ability to proactively share learning within the system, even if the organization ideally seems to support it. Conversely, there are also conditions within individuals that prevent their full participation in learning, even when asked to do so. These conditions include undue influence by managers or other powerful learner designates, including unions; lack of learning skills or developmental capability for organizational learning; and the changing social contract.

Undue Influence by Learner Designates. First, managers or others are often designated to learn on behalf of the organization. Their view of what should be learned acts as a funnel for what they think is in the organization's best interests, and therefore limits what people are able to learn. This can be damaging or discouraging to individual development. It can also be damaging to the creation of ideas that, in the long run, would benefit the system. Likely consequences include the loss of energy, enthusiasm, and good ideas of these young partners, who ostensibly had been hired to renew the lifeblood and thinking of the company. Senior managers, as learner designates, use their power to limit learning, not to enhance it.

The fruits of learning are typically valued more when they come from those who have more status, power, or influence—whether privilege is a function of formal authority or informal attribution. Advocates of both participatory democracy in the workplace (Lawler, 1986) and of chaos theory (Wheatley, 1993) suggest, for different reasons, that both individuals and organizations suffer when structures interfere with the widespread emergence, flow, and use of ideas. Position in the hierarchy or perceptions of privilege in society because of one's gender, race, or class often influence the availability of ideas or their degree of acceptance. This limits the role that individuals play in influencing organizational learning. In addition, people often censor their own contributions because of past experiences in this regard, whether or not such censorship is required. This leads to a collusion of silence; however, if people spoke up effectively, they might challenge taken-for-granted beliefs and strategies.

Power can be abused by employee representatives as well as by managers. Unions may encourage individuals to resist learning initiatives unless they are explicitly bargained agreements. Such action may well be justified in an antagonistic culture that is not truly oriented to learning or collaboration. However, it further feeds a culture of mistrust and may lead to self-fulfilling prophecies for both individuals and organizations.

Lack of Learning Skills or Developmental Capability. A second limitation is related; that is, that people do not always have the skills to learn well, as individuals or as agents for the organization. Nor have organizations historically been designed to support mutual inquiry and learning. In theory, the organization's norms and culture are socially constructed, which implies that everyone can influence these outcomes. However, even when people are willing and able to step outside the system and challenge it, they must be skillful in the way in which they communicate and challenge the thinking of others. Ground rules and expectations for these kinds of conversations are themselves influenced by prior socialization, which typically has occurred under a command-and-control hierarchy that inhibits open challenge.

Some developmental theorists (Fisher and Torbert, 1995; Kegan, 1994) suggest that everyone may not be developmentally able to understand systems-wide learning, and thus might find it difficult to proactively engage in it even when they wish to do so. Kegan and others suggest that many adults have not yet grown to the developmental level where they can, in fact, separate themselves from a situation enough to critique it (and the roles they and others play in creating and maintaining the status quo), let alone shape the situation toward new directions. Becoming aware of the way in which individual learning shapes organizational learning may well be a developmental task for which many are not yet sufficiently prepared.

Changing Social Contract. The old social contract in workplaces did not include a negotiated agreement around learning. Organizations often provided learning when they felt it met their needs, but they did not proactively encourage individuals to engage in learning, or value any learning other than that for which they saw immediate productivity gains. Individuals, as well as organizations, now need to unlearn this old frame of mind, and develop a mind-set that welcomes continuous learning on the part of individuals and the organization.

Field and Ford (1995) specifically address areas germane to the changing social contract that relate to the individual's own learning and the way in which individuals can influence organizational learning. Some of these include

- the enterprise's vision for the future, and the conceptual changes necessary to move in the direction of that vision
- specific changes in areas such as work organisation, skill formation, recognition and reward, and information management
- specific ways of monitoring and providing feedback (so that *goal-based learning* can occur) and a commitment to continual improvement (so that *learning through critical questioning* is recognised and supported). [p. 52; emphasis in original]

Conclusion

We thus return to the mystery of the lukasa as we reflect back on the ideas in this chapter. Individuals can act as learner designates and influence organizational learning, but only if conditions in the environment change to support them in this role and welcome their input. For learning to be effective, individuals must enable not only attention to the past, but also fresh insight into the present and future. And organizations must be able to open their doors to views that may, initially, seem to threaten their stability, yet by their very challenge, enable fresh ideas that feed enhancement of systems capacity.

References

Argyris, C., and Schön, D. *Organizational Learning II: Theory, Method, and Practice*. Reading, Mass.: Addison-Wesley, 1996.

Brookfield, S. D. *Understanding and Facilitating Adult Learning: A Comprehensive Analysis of Principles and Effective Practices*. San Francisco: Jossey-Bass Publishers, 1986.

Candy, P. *Self-Direction for Lifelong Learning: A Comprehensive Guide to Theory and Practice*. San Francisco: Jossey-Bass, 1991.

Dewey, J. *Experience and Education*. New York: Collier Books, 1938.

Field, L., and Ford, B. *Managing Organisational Learning: From Rhetoric to Reality*. Melbourne, Australia: Longman Australia, 1995.

Fisher, D., and Torbert, W. R. *Personal and Organizational Transformations: The True Challenge of Continual Quality Improvement*. London: McGraw-Hill, 1995.

Freire, P. *Pedagogy of the Oppressed*. New York: Seabury Press, 1974.

Jarvis, P. *Adult Learning in the Social Context*. London: Croom Helm, 1987.

Kegan, R. *In Over Our Heads: The Mental Demands of Modern Life*. Cambridge, Mass.: Harvard University Press, 1994.

Lawler, E. *High-Involvement Management: Participative Strategies for Improving Organizational Performance*. San Francisco: Jossey-Bass, 1986.

Mezirow, J. *Transformative Dimensions of Adult Learning*. San Francisco: Jossey-Bass, 1991.

Nooter, M. H. "Memory and the Mnemonic Arts." Paper presented at Columbia University, New York, October 1993.

Roberts, M. N. "Divination Board (*Lukasa*)." In T. Phillips (ed.), *Africa: The Art of a Continent*. New York: Prestel, 1996.

Rogers, C. *On Becoming a Person*. London: Constable, 1967.

Schön, D. A. *The Reflective Practitioner*. San Francisco: Jossey-Bass, 1983.

Watkins, K. E., and Marsick, V. J. *Sculpting the Learning Organization: Lessons in the Art and Science of Systematic Change*. San Francisco: Jossey-Bass, 1993.

Welton, M. R. (ed.). *In Defense of the Life World: Critical Perspectives on Adult Learning*. Albany: State University of New York Press, 1995.

Wheatley, M. *Leadership and the New Science*. San Francisco: Berrett-Koehler, 1993.

VICTORIA J. MARSICK is associate professor of adult education at Teachers College, Columbia University, and a consultant with both the Institute for Leadership in International Management and Partners for the Learning Organization.

PETER G. NEAMAN is a medical communications and marketing consultant who is also an amateur art historian and an M.A. student in organizational psychology at Teachers College, Columbia University.

CONCLUSION

Sustainable competitive advantage has proven elusive for companies in the 1990s. Although they have made enormous investments in technology, research, and state-of-the-art marketing, many of today's companies continue to ignore the single most important factor in achieving and maintaining competitive success: people. Companies with a highly committed workforce repeatedly outdistance their rivals in both profits and returns.

People and their learning are becoming more important because many other sources of competitive success are less powerful than they once were. Recognizing that the basis of competitive advantage has changed is essential to developing a different frame of reference for management and for corporate strategy. Traditional sources of success—product and process technology, protected or regulated markets, access to financial resources, and economies of scale—can still provide competitive leverage, but to a lesser degree now than in the past, leaving organizational culture and capabilities, derived from people and workplace learning, as comparatively more vital.

If competitive success is achieved through people, then the skills of those people are critical. Consequently, one of the most obvious implications of the changing basis of competitive success is the growing importance of having a workforce with adequate skills. Between 1929 and 1982, education prior to work accounted for 26 percent of the growth in the productive capacity of the United States, with learning on the job contributing to an additional 55 percent (Carnevale and Goldstein, 1990). Carnevale and Goldstein go on to say that "learning in school and learning on the job are by far the most important factors behind American economic growth and productivity in this century, and will determine the nation's economic prospects in the next"(p. 30).

Throughout our lives, learning experiences are an important source of personal stimulation. Workplace learning represents a positive hope, both for people first entering the world of work and for individuals changing their work environments. Employees must learn to anticipate rapid change in their jobs, careers, work groups, and organizations. Farsightedness is learned. Adult education-human resource development (HRD) can contribute to this learning by basing organized training, education, individual development, and organization development on expected future needs when appropriate to do so. Before workplace learning can help propel organizations into the next century, those engaged in aiding the process must refine and define the nature of their work.

This volume has attempted to further the process of refining and redefining the field by exploring some of the issues associated with helping adults to learn in the workplace. Looking across all the issues, some generalizations about the state of the art of workplace learning can be made. Those generalizations are that the field is trying to forge an identity for itself, practitioners of workplace learning are concerned with professionalization of the field, and there are some new and emerging issues facing educators of adults in the workplace.

Forging an Identity

When you consider that what most acknowledge as the foundations of the modern world of work, as we know it, didn't emerge until early this century (Frederick Taylor in 1911; Henri Fayol in 1929; and Max Weber in 1936), it is easy to see that contemporary organizations are in their infancy. It is more difficult to see that a field of study that has been around since the building of the pyramids, as Willis described in her chapter, could still be in its infancy as well. Nevertheless, whereas workplace learning continues to grow in its importance to organizations, the field of study seems to be in its adolescence, at best. As with any adolescent, one of the most critical issues at hand is to forge an identity; to find out who we are and who we will become.

Those who help adults to learn in the workplace are struggling with just these issues—what is our purpose and where did we come from? Willis believes that, like professionals in a lot of other disciplines, we have drawn from many fields and have merged them all together like the tributaries of the Mississippi River flow together to form a mighty confluence. In her view, HRD stands apart from other disciplines and has, in fact, established its identity separate from other fields like psychology, human resource management, and adult education. Dirkx, on the other hand, feels that HRD has separated itself from adult education only through its focus on the bottom line; that adult education is the same whether it occurs in the workplace, the community center, or the formal classroom.

The focus on the bottom line is what Swanson and Arnold feel defines HRD. They espouse the view that the only reason for conducting workplace learning is to improve employee performance, thus allowing the organization to continue profitable operations. Bierema disagrees with their view and asserts that the purpose of workplace learning is to develop the individual, and that, in turn, will lead to more productive workplaces. Clearly, human capital defines one approach, whereas a more humanistic perspective underlies the other. Which of these views are right? It depends on one's perspective. These are the type of debates that help a young, fledgling field define itself.

Professionalization of the Field

As Ellinger and Gilley discuss, the people who are involved with educating adults in the workplace are concerned with professionalization and licensing. This concern is also indicative of an emerging field. Professional licensing can be seen either as a mechanism to set minimum standards of performance, or as a way to make the profession seem more elite and limit participation.

There is a legitimate concern that professionalization will limit participation. If a supervisor wishes to conduct a short training class on a new piece of equipment, does that mean that she or he would be barred from doing so without a license to conduct workplace learning sessions? Could a licensed practitioner be held liable for providing erroneous or dated information to a group of learners, much as a physician or engineer is? Closely tied to these questions and part-and-parcel to professionalization is the question of where the information base of a profession should come from. Professionalization involves having a specialized knowledge base that can be passed on to others—that one can be certified as knowing in order to practice.

Learning in the workplace is seen by many as a field of practitioners. Historically, many of the people engaged in adult education and HRD began in other disciplines and sort of "backed" their way into being facilitators of workplace learning. Often, these people were acknowledged as good practitioners in their respective trades and were asked by their employers to show others how to perform the same duties. Mott writes that this form of experience is what comes into play with a reflective practitioner. She feels that this type of reflective practitioner activity should be encouraged and will lead to a successful and professionalized field.

Chalofsky believes that if facilitators of workplace learning are ever to be taken seriously, their practice must have a solid foundation in research. This solid knowledge base, he contends, can only be built through systematic inquiry and not through trial and error. Much as research-based knowledge transformed healers from being seen as witch doctors to being seen as physicians, a solid research-based knowledge foundation is needed for facilitators of workplace learning to be viewed as professionals.

Regardless of the stance one takes concerning professionalization of the field, debates about such issues as licensing and derivation of the knowledge base are yet added indicators of the search for identity the field faces. Mature professions do not generally face these issues—they have long since been worked out. Nevertheless, facilitators of workplace learning are currently struggling with these issues.

Emerging Trends

Looking at how a field handles hot new topics or trends can go a long way toward determining its maturity level. The current hot topic in workplace learning is the Learning Organization. Marsick and Watkins square off over the issue of whether it is the organization that learns or whether it is actually individuals in organizations that do the learning. They each make a convincing case, but regardless of where one comes down on the issue, it still leaves one wondering—is this truly the defining moment for those who facilitate learning in the workplace? Have we finally found our niche? Is this the framework that will finally cause managers to realize the value to their organizations of workplace learning? Many in the field would answer these questions in the affirmative.

Still, there are others that are not quite so sure. They would point to other programs that not too long ago were seen as the savior of the field. Such programs as total quality management (TQM), quality of work life (QWL), and just-in-time-*whatever* were hailed as the defining moment of HRD. Although each of these programs may still be around in one form or the other and certainly have made their contributions to the workplace, there are many that would label them as passing fads.

Will the Learning Organization join its predecessors in the great bone yard of workplace fads or will it truly be the defining truth for HRD? If the Learning Organization does continue its current role as champion of workplace learning, how will you know if you have one? If the concept truly becomes deep-rooted, how will the workplace respond? We don't have the answers to these and many more questions—yet. As the field continues to struggle through its adolescence, that is, defining what it is and where it is going, these and many more questions will continue to arise.

Where does HRD-adult education in the workplace go from here? What will be the hot new topics coming down the pike? What is on the horizon? No one can know for sure what the future holds. Some things we do know are already beginning to emerge. For example, diversity training is gaining a lot of attention lately. As the nature of the workforce in the United States continues to change, those charged with aiding learning in the workplace are being asked to accomplish what society has struggled with for many years. Will we have any more success than society as a whole has had? We know that even a degree of success in this area will not be the last hurdle to cross before the field is defined—we are already beginning to talk about globalization of the workplace.

How will the development and education of workers fit into a global economy? As other cultures establish business concerns in the United States, will they adapt to our concept of workplace learning, or will we adapt to theirs—or are they the same thing? How will the introduction of other values change our perception of the value of learning? Or, as U.S. companies spread out globally, will we carry our ideals to other cultures, and perhaps, some might say, pollute them? Just what effect will the mingling and merging of multiple cultures have on those who facilitate workplace learning?

Finally, what may become one of the most critical issues to face educators of adults in the workplace is one of social consciousness. Authors such as Kincheloe (1995) and Korten (1996) contend that workplace learning should include an explicit focus on the social and ethical issues of work. They call for the education and training of workers who are not only skilled in communicating, problem solving, acquiring and using information, and developing the capacity to be lifelong learners but are aware of the past traditions and current status of workers' rights movements as well. Kincheloe calls for problem-centered training that addresses various themes, including "the environment; the quest for justice; the fragility of democracy; poverty and economic development; the quest for peace; problems of technology, transportation, hunger, and nutrition;

urban decay; and violence" (p. 286). He argues that these issues of democracy and the corporation's place in it have been quickly forgotten in the scramble to compete globally.

Will this be the new challenge for educators of adults in the workplace? Just as the workplace has been called on to correct the deficiencies of the public education system in literacy and numeracy education, will it be called on to correct deficiencies in social consciousness? How will corporate stakeholders respond? Even if this concept catches on in the United States, how will it play out in global workplaces—would nondemocratic host countries even allow the introduction of such ideas to a local workforce? Are the current educators of adults in the workplace equipped for this type of an undertaking? It will be interesting to watch the answers to these questions unfold.

To quote an often overused axiom—so many questions, so few answers. But, it is the exploration of issues such as the ones addressed in this volume that causes a field to develop, grow, and mature, much as an adolescent does as he or she moves toward young adulthood. We hope you have gained some insights from *Workplace Learning: Debating Five Critical Questions of Theory and Practice.* Speaking on behalf of all the contributors, we hope you have enjoyed this volume. It has been our pleasure to address some of the issues concerning the facilitation of workplace learning, and to suggest some new issues that may warrant debate in a future volume. For it is this type of scholarly debate that will help us refine and define the field, and perhaps help move the field from adolescence to young adulthood—or further.

Robert W. Rowden
Editor

References

Carnevale, A., and Goldstein, H. "Schooling and Training for Work in America: An Overview." In L. Ferman, M. Hoyman, J. Cutcher-Gershenfeld, and E. Savoie (eds.), *New Developments in Worker Training: A Legacy for the 1990s.* Madison, Wis.: Industrial Relations Research Association, 1990.

Kincheloe, J. *Toil and Trouble: Good Work, Smart Workers, and the Integration of Academic and Vocational Education.* New York: Peter Lang, 1995.

Korten, D. *When Corporations Rule the World.* San Francisco: Berrett-Koehler, 1996.

INDEX

Academy for Human Resource Development, 54–55
Academy of Management, 55
Accreditation, 76. *See also* Certification
Ackoff, R., 21
Action learning, 37
Action model, of HRD, 36
Action science, 59
Adult education: assumptions of, 44; costs of, 3; democratic goal of, 42, 44; HRD and, 4–6, 16–18, 36–37, 41–42, 44–46; performance improvement and, 16; productivity and, 105; training and, 4; triangle model of, 58–59; workplace and, 3. *See also* Adult learning
Adult Education Quarterly, 58
Adult learners, 36
Adult learning: andragogy and, 44–45; change in nature of, 3; holistic development and, 25; meaning making and, 99, 101; organizational change and, 92; organizational learning and, 90–91, 97, 101–103. *See also* Adult education; Self-directed learning (SDL)
Adult learning theory: contextual influences and, 101; humanistic focus of, 99; individual focus of, 101; organizational learning and, 99–101; problem-solving model of, 100; scientific method and, 100; self-directed learning focus of, 99
American Assocation for Adult Education, 4
American Society for Training and Development (ASTD), 5, 52, 67, 72, 78, 80
American Society for Training Performance and Instruction (ASTPI), 71
Andragogy, 6, 44–45
Argyris, C., 89, 90, 91, 98, 100, 101

Baird, L. S., 31
Banathy, B., 34
Bedrick, R., 71
Bergevin, P., 27
Bertalanffy, L. von, 34, 35
Bion, W., 89
Block, P., 26
Bohm, D., 21

Booth, B., 76, 80
Boundary spanning, 93
Bratton, B., 70, 76
Bridges, W., 79
Brockcank, W., 79
Brookfield, S. D., 42, 45, 46, 57, 58, 99
Brown, S. M., 59, 61
Bullett, F., 68

Caffarella, R., 24, 25, 41
Campbell, J., 7
Candy, P. C., 24, 99
Capra, F., 21, 22, 23, 24
Carlson, R., 7
Carnevale, A. P., 3, 79, 93, 105
Carnevale, E. S., 79
Carr, W., 58
Cascio, W. F., 14
Certificate programs, 77–78
Certification programs: certificate programs and, 77; growth of, 76, 78; in HRD, 77–78; in HRM, 77; human resource training and development, 77–78; traditional vs. nontraditional, 77–78
Certification: accredication and, 76; administrative/regulatory issues and, 82; arguments against, 80–81; arguments for, 81–83; body of knowledge and, 81; debate about, 7, 76; definitions of, 76; individual advantages of, 82; licensure and, 76; official organizations for, 72; organizational advantages of, 82; positive implications of, 82–83; professional advantages of, 82–83; professionalization and, 76; qualification and, 76; restrictions of labor supply and, 81–82; workplace trends and, 78–80. *See also* Professionalization
Cervero, R. M., 7, 58, 72, 76
Chalofsky, N., 36, 53, 55
Change: cyclical process of, 62; individual learning and, 92; organizational culture and, 92, 94; organizational learning and, 90
Chaos theory, 102
Cherrington, D. J., 77
Cohen, S., 6

Collins, M., 42, 45, 70, 76
Competencies, 69–70
Competitive advantage, 79, 105
Confluence of systems, in HRD, 32–33
Continuous learning, 8, 103
Cook, W., 3
Coscarelli, W., 76, 80
Courtney, S., 41
Cram, D. D., 68, 69, 72, 73
Cranton, P., 5
Credentialing: employability and, 79; HRD development and, 67; terminology about, 76–77. *See also* Certification; Professional licensure; Professionalization
Crossan, M. M., 27
Cunningham, P. M., 42, 45

Democratization: adult education goal of, 44; organizational learning and, 94; quality improvement effort and, 44; self-managed teams and, 44–45; workplace, 44
Deqey, J., 22, 24, 25
Deshler, D., 58
Dewey, J., 60, 100
Diversity: of HRD, 69, 72; practitioner, 80; of work force, 108
Diversity training, 18, 108
Dixon, N., 52, 55
Djurfeldt, L., 27
Dodgson, M., 26

Educational Researcher, 58
Educative workplace, 45–46
Eggland, S. A., 42, 67, 71
Elfenbein, M. J., 59, 61
Embeddedness, 91
Employee development: context of, 22–23; economics of, 24–25; holistic, 25; individual growth and, 25; mechanistic world view and, 22–23; organizational culture and, 26; organizational hierarchy and, 26; organizational infrastructure and, 25; personal mastery and, 25; personalized, 26; productivity and, 24; self-direction and, 24. *See also* Individual development
Empowerment, 93–94
Ethics, 71. *See also* Social consciousness
Evolutionary systems thinking, 35. *See also* Systems thinking
Executive, 55

Field, L., 103
File cabinet model, of HRD, 37–38
Filipczak, B., 75, 80
Fiol, M. C., 89, 90
Fisher, D., 102
Flood, R. L., 35, 36
Ford, B., 103
Fordham, F., 89
Freire, P., 99
Friedson, E., 7
Fritz, R., 26
"Future of Workplace Learning and Performance, The," 3

Gaioner, L., 93
Galbraith, M. W., 7, 67, 70, 72, 76, 80, 81, 88
Gaudet, C. H., 78
Geis, G., 69–70
Gerhart, B., 14
Gill, S. J., 15
Gilley, J. W., 7, 42, 67, 68, 69–70, 71, 72, 76, 80, 81, 88
Globalization, 108–109
Goal-based learning, 103
Goldstein, H., 105
Goldstein, I., 7
Group intelligence, 89
Groupthink, 89

Hagan, N., 58
Handy, C., 79
Hart, M. U., 42, 45
Heider, F., 93
Henkelman, J., 52, 53
Hildebrand, M., 70, 76
Hochberger, J., 81
Hollenbeck, J. R., 14
Holt, M. E., 76, 77, 78
HRD models, 35–37, 44–45, 52–53
Human performance technology, 6
Human resource development (HRD): adult education and, 4–6, 16–18, 36–37, 41–42, 44–46; as applied discipline, 52; definitions of, 16; development of, 6–8, 51, 70; evolutionary systems thinking and, 33–35; file cabinet of, 37–38; goals of, 13, 15; HRM and, 35–36; human resource costs and, 14; individual development approach to, 13; knowledge base of, 6–7, 52, 71; learning organization and, 8; major perspectives on, 36; market economy and,

42–44; mechanistic approach of, 22, 45; new identity for, 106; performance approach and, 13, 16–19, 32–33; root disciplines of, 32–33; as subsystem, 14–15; systems redesign of, 36–38; systems thinking and, 23, 32–34; workplace democratization and, 42; workplace fads in, 18, 108. *See also* Practice; Practitioners; Professionalization; Research; Standards; Theory; Training; *specific HRD models*

Human Resource Development Quarterly, 54, 58

Human resource management (HRM): certification programs in, 77; HRD and, 6, 35–36

Human resource wheel model, of HRD, 35

Individual development: crisis in, 23–24; framework for, 24–27; holistic approach to, 22, 24–25; learning organization and, 22; new paradigm of, 22; organizational development and, 25; performance and, 26; systems model of, 25; workplace learning and, 106. *See also* Employee development

Individual growth and development approach, 6

Individual learning. *See* Adult learning

Instructional systems design (ISD), 34

Instructor Competencies, 69

International Board of Standards for Training, Performance, and Instruction (IBSTPI), 71–72, 80, 82

International Society of Performance and Instruction (ISPI), 71

Jacobs, R., 18, 52, 53

James, W., 7, 76, 80, 81

Janis, I. L., 89

Jarvis, P., 23, 52

Jenne, J. T., 58

Jensen, G., 52

Just-in-time work force, 79

Kaeter, M., 80

Kahn, R. L., 14

Katz, D., 14

Kegan, R., 102

Keith, J., 6

Kemmis, S., 58

Kidd, J. R., 55

Kincheloe, J. L., 42, 43, 44, 45, 108

Knowledge base, of HRD, 6–7, 52, 55, 71, 81

Knowles, M., 6, 23, 44

Korten, D., 24, 108

Kotrlik, J. W., 78

Kottkamp, R. B., 61

Kuhn, T. S., 35

Laird, D., 31

Lake, D. G., 79

Lane, H. W., 27

Lapides, J., 78, 80

Lapp, H. J., 76

Laszlo, E., 35

Latham, G., 4, 7

Lawler, E., 102

Learned helplessness, 93

Learning: making space for, 93–94; performance and, 27; power and, 98, 102; social context of, 99; social contract and, 103. *See also* Adult education; Adult learning; Continuous learning; Goal-based learning; Organizational learning; Self-directed learning (SDL); Whole-person learning; Workplace learning

Learning at the rate of change (LRC), 33

Learning cycle, 91–93

Learning organization: conditions of growth in, 22; cooperation and control in, 99; definition of, 8, 18, 91; HRD and, 8; individual development and, 22; individual meaning making and, 99, 101; as new trend, 107; paradox of, 98; performance improvement and, 18; research and development in, 93; saving the gains and, 91; slack and, 93; social impact of, 22

Learning pyramid, 25

Learning through critical questioning, 103

Lee, C., 72, 76

Leonard, B., 77

Levering, R., 14

Lewin, K., 59, 93

Lewinian model of social science, 59

Licensure, 76. *See also* Certification; Professional licensure

Lincoln, C., 36, 53

Lindeman, E. C., 4, 41, 44

Locus of control, 16–17

Lopos, G. J., 76, 77

Luba, 97–98

Lukasa, 97–98
Lyles, M. A., 89, 90

McCullough, R. C., 80
McLagan, P. A., 16, 35, 52, 53, 69–70, 71, 79
Mager, R. F., 68, 69, 72, 73
Manager Competencies, 69
Managers, HRD, 5, 101–102
March, J. G., 89, 91
Market economy model, of HRD, 43–44
Marsick, V. J., 24, 26, 36, 45, 62, 79, 89, 91, 100
May, G. L., 36
Mechanistic world view: HRD and, 22; individual development and, 23–24; influence of, 21; organizations and, 23; paradigm shift and, 21–22; workplace learning and, 22, 26
Merriam, S., 24, 25, 41, 55
Merrill, K., 81
Methaphor model, of HRD, 36
Meyer, A., 89, 91
Mezirow, J., 45, 99, 100, 101
Miller, E. L., 68
Mills, D., 70
Mills, G. E., 3, 35
Morgan, G., 91
Morrow, L., 79
Moskowitz, M., 14
Motivation, 93
Mott, V. W., 60
Mumford, A., 25
Murphy, B., 58, 59

Nadler, L., 27, 42, 51
Nadler, Z., 27
National Coalition for Advanced Manufacturing, 6
National Society for Performance and Instruction (NSPI), 78
"1995 Industry Report," 3, 79
Noe, R. A., 14
Nonaka, I., 79, 90
Nooter, M. H., 97
Nordquist, H. E., 21

Olsen, J. P., 89, 91
Organizational culture: change and, 92; performance improvement and, 16; systems thinking and, 26
Organizational development: change in, 26; individual development and, 25;

learning pyramid and, 25; productivity and, 33; stage theory of, 70
Organizational learning: adult learning theory and, 99–101; autonomy and, 94; change and, 90; collaborative structures and, 93; conditions of, 90, 93; embeddedness and, 91; employee empowerment and, 93; feedback and, 103; freedom and, 93–94; group intelligence and, 89; individual action for, 94–95; individual learning and, 90–91, 97; individual role in, 101–103; learner designates' influence and, 101–102. learning cycle theory and, 91–92; management strategy and, 103; motivation and, 93; new management approaches and, 90; organizational change and, 92; organizational culture and, 92, 94; organizational knowledge creation and, 90; organizational memory and, 91; organizational support for, 94–95; organizational triggers for, 91–92; organizational vision and, 103; paradox of, 98–99; perceptions of privilege and, 102; power and, 102; skills/developmental capacity and, 102; slack and, 93; social contract and, 103; socialization and, 99–100; software programs and, 94; systems influencing, 93; technology and, 91; understanding, 89. *See also* Workplace learning
Organizational memory: embedded learning and, 91; lukasa example of, 97–98
Organizational performance. *See* Performance
Organizational structure, shamrock model of, 79
Organizations: definition of, 14–15, 91; goals of business, 14; HRD as subsystem of, 14–15; human resources in, 14; infrastructure of, 26; learning cycle and, 91–92; locus of control in, 16–17; mechanistic world view and, 23; mission of, 16; performance and, 15
Osterberg, R. V., 26
Osterman, K. F., 61
Outsourcing, 79–80

Pace, R. W., 3, 35
Participatory democracy, 102. *See also* Democratization
Patton, E., 6
Performance: definition of, 15; HRD and, 15–18; individual development and,

26; learning and, 27; levels of, 15; measures of, 15; universal standards for, 80; workplace learning and, 21, 106
Performance improvement: adult education and, 16; HRD and, 16–17; as HRD discipline, 32; learning organization and, 18; organizational culture/mission and, 16; workplace learning and, 6; training and, 33
Performance Improvement Quarterly, 54
Performance vs. learning debate, 17
Personnel Accreditation Institute (PAI), 72
Peters, T. J., 59, 61
Posititivist view of knowledge, 58
Power, learning and, 98, 102
Practice: client wants and, 54; confidence crisis and, 61; contextual demands and, 59; guesswork and, 54; state of art and, 54; theories-in-use and, 60; theory and, 54–55, 57–61. *See also* Theory-practice relationship
Practice-oriented research: classroom needs and, 62; factors affecting, 58; legitimacy of, 58; need for, 57; professional practice and, 59–61; promotion of, 61–62; reflective theory building and, 58–62; theory-practice relationship and, 58–59
Practitioners: background experience of, 107; certification of, 7; diversity among, 80; environmental challenges for, 59; proficiency testing of, 71–72; research needs of, 55. *See also* Competencies
Problem-centered training, 108–109
Productivity: education and, 105; individual development and, 24; organizational development and, 33
Profession: classifications of, 67–68; definition of, 68; essential characteristics of, 71
Professional licensure: diversity/extensiveness of field and, 69, 81; divisiveness of, 69; evaluation issues and, 69; informal approach to, 72–73; lack of need for, 69; negative implications of, 68–69, 72–73, 80–81; purposes of, 68; regulation of field and, 68. *See also* Certification
Professionalization: certification and, 76; certifying organizations and, 71–72; characteristic orientation and, 70–71; components of, 7; failure of, 53–54; knowledge base and, 52–53, 81, 107;

limited participation and, 107; looseness of field and, 72; nontraditional orientation on, 72–73; occupational classifications and, 67–68; perspectives on, 70, 73; philosophical orientation and, 70; practitioner certification and, 7; process of, 69–72; research/practice and, 55; role/competency model and, 52–53; science and, 59; structuring of field and, 52; theoretical basis of, 55; workplace learning and, 7–8. *See also* Professional licensure
Proficiency testing, 71

Qualification, 76. *See also* Certification
Quality improvement, 44
Quality of work life (QWL), 108

Reality, new vision of, 22
Reflection, 60
Reflection-for-action, 60
Reflective theory building: inquiry/investigation and, 61; practice-oriented research and, 58–62; process of, 60–61; promotion of, 61; reflection-for-action and, 60
Reinhart, C., 55
Research: antagonism toward, 57, 61; deficits in, 54; need for, 55; practitioner complaints about, 57; practitioners and, 55; quarterly hierarchy and, 58; theory-practice debate and, 58. *See also* Practice-oriented research
Revans, R., 33
Roberts, M. N., 97, 98
Rogers, C., 59, 99
Role/competency model, of HRD, 52–53
Rothwell, W., 7

Saving the gains, 91
Scheer, W. E., 71
Schneier, C. E., 31
Schön, D., 7, 60, 61, 89, 90, 91, 98, 99, 100, 101
Schultz, E., 3
Self-directed learning (SDL): adult learning theory and, 99; adult propensity for, 25; humanistic aspect of, 6; statistics on, 24. *See also* Adult learning
Self-managed teams, 44–45
Senge, P., 8, 18, 22, 23, 25, 26, 34, 92
Settle, T. J., 17
Seyfer, C., 69–70

Shamrock model, of organizational structure, 79
Sisco, B. R., 67
Slack, 93
Smith, P. C., 3, 35
Smith, T. R., 77, 78, 81
Social consciousness, 108–109. *See also* Ethics
Social contract, 104
Social science, Lewinian model of, 59
Society for General Systems Research, 34
Society for Human Resource Management (SHRM), 71
Sork, T. J., 69, 72
Sredl, H., 7
Standards: certification and, 7; competencies and, 69–70; ethics and, 71; universal performance, 80
Stata, R., 79
Students, 62
Suhadolnik, D., 69–70, 71
Swanson, R., 4, 6, 15, 16, 17, 35
Synergy, 32
Systematic thinking, 34
Systemic organizational learning (SOL), 33
Systemic thinking, 34. *See also* Systems thinking
Systems-level learning, 101
Systems theory: confluence analogy of, 32; HRD and, 34; metalevel function of, 35; methodological positions of, 35; synergy and, 32 classification system for, 34; developmetal limitations and, 102; freedom of movement and, 94; goal of, 22; HRD and, 23, 32–33; individual development and, 25; learning organization and, 23; legitimation of, 34–35; organizational culture and, 26; organizational learning and, 27. *See also* Evolutionary systems thinking

Taylor, E., 43
Team building, 18
Teams. *See* Self-managed teams
Terkel, S., 43
Theories-in-use, 60
Theory: practice and, 52, 54–55, 57–61; research and, 55; systems approach to, 34; value of, 57. *See also* HRD models; Knowledge base, of HRD; Reflective theory building; Theories-in-use; Theory-practice relationship; *and specific models*
Theory-practice relationship: action science and, 59; positivist view of knowledge and, 58; practice-based research and, 58; triangle model of, 58–59
Torbert, W. R., 102
Torraco, R., 4, 6, 15
Total quality management (TQM), 108
Training: adult education and, 4; costs of, 3; expenditures on, 79–80; history of, 4–6; HRD and, 16–17; outsourcing of, 79–80; performance technology and, 33; statistics, 41; wartime, 5. *See also* Diversity training; Problem-centered training
Training and Development, 55
"Trends That Will Influence Workplace Learning," 79, 80
Triangle model, of adult education, 58–59

Ulrich, D., 79
Underwood, L P., 31
United States Department of Education, 41

Villet, J., 93
Vollmer, H., 70

Wanniski, J., 42
Waterman, R. H., 59, 61
Watkins, K., 4, 17, 24, 26, 35, 36, 42, 45, 53, 59, 61, 62, 79, 81, 89, 91, 100
Welock, B. A., 69, 72
Welton, M. R., 45
Welton, R. 99
Wexley, K., 4
Wheatley, M., 21, 35, 102
White, B., 7, 76, 80
White, R. E., 27
Whole-person learning, 27. *See also* Individual development
Whole-system model, of HRD, 37
Whyte, G. S., 70
Wiley, C., 75, 76, 77, 78, 80, 81
Wilkinson, E. S., Jr., 75
Willis, V., 35, 36, 42, 53,
Work: foundations of, 106; humanistic view of, 45; new paradigm of, 44; redefining, 105
Workforce: competitive advantage and, 105; contingent, 79; diversity in, 108; education level of, 6
Workplace: certification and, 78–80; competitive advantage in, 79, 105; contingent workforce and, 79; democratization of, 42; educative model of, 45–46; historical changes in, 4–5; learning empha-

sis in, 79; nature of adult education and, 3; new paradigm in, 44; outsourcing and, 79–80; participatory democracy in, 102; program fads in, 108; quality improvement effort in, 44; social contract in, 103; trends in, 78–80; universal performance standards and, 80

Workplace education: future direction of, 108; globalization and, 108; social consciousness and, 108–109

Workplace learning: adult education and, 4; andragogical prinicples of, 44–45; competitive advantage and, 79; competitive system and, 23; context of, 22–23; Dewey's contribution to, 100; emerging trends in, 107–109; employee development and, 22–23; generalizations about, 105–106; history of, 4–6; hope of, 105; HRD approach to, 5–6; identity of HRD and, 106; individual development and, 106; individual growth and development approach to, 6; learning cycle theory and, 91–92; learning pyramid and, 25; mechanistic world view and, 22, 26; new models of, 27; new world view and, 21; organizational infrastructure and, 26; performance and, 21, 27; performance improvement approach to, 6; performance view of, 106; as practitioner oriented, 107; purpose of, 5–6; redefining work and, 105; systems model of, 27; systems thinking and, 22; unintentional, 24; views of, 5–6. *See also* Organizational learning

World view: individual development and, 22; paradigm shift in, 21–22; systems-oriented, 22. *See also* Mechanistic world view

Wright, P. M., 14

Yeung, A. K., 79

ORDERING INFORMATION

NEW DIRECTIONS FOR ADULT AND CONTINUING EDUCATION is a series of paperback books that explores issues of common interest to instructors, administrators, counselors, and policy makers in a broad range of adult and continuing education settings—such as colleges and universities, extension programs, businesses, the military, prisons, libraries, and museums. Books in the series are published quarterly in Spring, Summer, Fall, and Winter and are available for purchase by subscription and individually.

SUBSCRIPTIONS cost $52.00 for individuals (a savings of 35 percent over single-copy prices) and $79.00 for institutions, agencies, and libraries. Standing orders are accepted. New York residents, add local sales tax for subscriptions. (For subscriptions outside the United States, add $7.00 for shipping via surface mail or $25.00 for air mail. Orders *must be prepaid* in U.S. dollars by check drawn on a U.S. bank or charged to VISA, MasterCard, or American Express.)

SINGLE COPIES cost $20.00 plus shipping (see below) when payment accompanies order. California, New Jersey, New York, and Washington, D.C., residents, please include appropriate sales tax. Canadian residents, add GST and any local taxes. Billed orders will be charged shipping and handling. No billed shipments to post office boxes. (Orders from outside the United States *must be prepaid* in U.S. dollars by check drawn on a U.S. bank or charged to VISA, MasterCard, or American Express.)

SHIPPING (SINGLE COPIES ONLY): $20.00 and under, add $3.50; to $50.00, add $4.50; to $75.00, add $5.50; to $100.00, add $6.50; to $150.00, add $7.50; over $150.00, add $8.50.

ALL PRICES are subject to change.

DISCOUNTS FOR QUANTITY ORDERS are available. Please write to the address below for information.

ALL ORDERS must include either the name of an individual or an official purchase order number. Please submit your order as follows:
   Subscriptions: specify series and year subscription is to begin
   Single copies: include individual title code (such as ACE 59)

MAIL ALL ORDERS TO:
   Jossey-Bass Publishers
   350 Sansome Street
   San Francisco, California 94104-1342

FOR SUBSCRIPTION SALES OUTSIDE OF THE UNITED STATES, contact any international subscription agency or Jossey-Bass directly.

OTHER TITLES AVAILABLE IN THE
NEW DIRECTIONS FOR ADULT AND CONTINUING EDUCATION SERIES
Ralph G. Brockett, Susan Imel, Editors-in-Chief
Alan B. Knox, Consulting Editor

ACE71   Learning in Groups: Exploring Fundamental Principles, New Uses, and
         Emerging Opportunities, *Susan Imel*
ACE70   A Community-Based Approach to Literacy Programs: Taking Learners'
         Lives into Account, *Peggy A. Sissel*
ACE69   What Really Matters in Adult Education Program Planning: Lessons in
         Negotiating Power and Interests, *Ronald M. Cervero, Arthur L. Wilson*
ACE68   Workplace Learning, *W. Franklin Spikes*
ACE67   Facilitating Distance Education, *Mark H. Rossman, Maxine E. Rossman*
ACE66   Mentoring: New Strategies and Challenges, *Michael W. Galbraith,
         Norman H. Cohen*
ACE65   Learning Environments for Women's Adult Development:
         Bridges Toward Change, *Kathleen Taylor, Catherine Marienau*
ACE64   Overcoming Resistance to Self-Direction in Adult Learning,
         Roger Hiemstra, Ralph G. Brockett
ACE63   The Emerging Power of Action Inquiry Technologies, *Ann Brooks,
         Karen E. Watkins*
ACE62   Experiential Learning: A New Approach, *Lewis Jackson,
         Rosemary S. Caffarella*
ACE61   Confronting Racism and Sexism, *Elisabeth Hayes, Scipio A. J. Colin III*
ACE60   Current Perspectives on Administration of Adult Education Programs,
         Patricia Mulcrone
ACE59   Applying Cognitive Learning Theory to Adult Learning, *Daniele D. Flannery*
ACE58   The Adult Educator as Consultant, *Lois J. Zachary, Sally Vernon*
ACE57   An Update on Adult Learning Theory, *Sharan B. Merriam*
ACE56   Rethinking Leadership in Adult and Continuing Education, *Paul J. Edelson*
ACE55   Professionals' Ways of Knowing: New Findings on How to Improve
         Professional Education, *H. K. Morris Baskett, Victoria J. Marsick*
ACE54   Confronting Controversies in Challenging Times: A Call for Action,
         Michael W. Galbraith, Burton R. Sisco
ACE53   Learning for Personal Development, *Lorraine A. Cavaliere, Angela Sgroi*
ACE52   Perspectives on Educational Certificate Programs, *Margaret E. Holt,
         George J. Lopos*
ACE51   Professional Development for Educators of Adults, *Ralph G. Brockett*
ACE50   Creating Environments for Effective Adult Learning, *Roger Hiemstra*
ACE49   Mistakes Made and Lessons Learned: Overcoming Obstacles to Successful
         Program Planning, *Thomas J. Sork*
ACE48   Serving Culturally Diverse Populations, *Jovita M. Ross-Gordon,
         Larry G. Martin, Diane Buck Briscoe*
ACE47   Education Through Community Organizations, *Michael W. Galbraith*
ACE45   Applying Adult Development Strategies, *Mark H. Rossman, Maxine E. Rossman*
CE44   Fulfilling the Promise of Adult and Continuing Education, *B. Allan Quigley*
CE43   Effective Teaching Styles, *Elisabeth Hayes*
CE42   Participatory Literacy Education, *Arlene Fingeret, Paul Jurmo*
CE41   Recruiting and Retaining Adult Students, *Peter S. Cookson*
CE32   Issues in Adult Career Counseling, *Juliet V. Miller, Mary Lynne Musgrove*
CE31   Marketing Continuing Education, *Hal Beder*
CE25   Self-Directed Learning: From Theory to Practice, *Stephen Brookfield*
CE22   Designing and Implementing Effective Workshops, *Thomas J. Sork*
CE19   Helping Adults Learn How to Learn, *Robert M. Smith*